Escape Average

GO FOR THE

BIG

It's Time to Break through What's Stopping You

By

Michael Botts

Published by Best Seller Publishing®, Pasadena, CA
Best Seller Publishing® is a registered trademark
Printed in the United States of America.

This publication is designed to provide accurate and authoritative information with regard to the subject matter covered. It is sold with the understanding that the publisher is not engaged in rendering legal, accounting, or other professional advice. If legal advice or other expert assistance is required, the services of a competent professional should be sought. The opinions expressed by the authors in this book are not endorsed by Best Seller Publishing® and are the sole responsibility of the author rendering the opinion.

Most Best Seller Publishing® titles are available at special quantity discounts for bulk purchases for sales promotions, premiums, fundraising, and educational use. Special versions or book excerpts can also be created to fit specific needs.

For more information, please write:
Best Seller Publishing®
1346 Walnut Street, #205
Pasadena, CA 91106
or call 1(626) 765 9750
Toll Free: 1(844) 850-3500
Visit us online at: www.BestSellerPublishing.org

Table of Contents

INTRODUCTION

Remember when you could dream big and spectacular dreams? You could give every detail and talk about it for hours with an excitement that kept your heart pounding out of your chest late into the night just from thinking about it? Remember how limitless your thinking was? Remember the smile in your soul as you lay there, staring through the ceiling of your bedroom into the life you were going to live?

And now the thing you get most excited about is the weekend, or the kid's soccer game, or the two-week vacation you will spend at your mother-in-law's house because you can't afford to go on your dream vacation.

That's the state of mind I was in one day as I sat on the toilet in my house, 90 days late on the mortgage with foreclosure letters piled up on my dining room table. As I sat there scrolling through other people's highlights, trying to mute the scream in my soul, I heard my four kids—Elijah, 9; Mikayla, 7; Noah, 4; and Caleb, 3—shouting, "Daddy, somebody is in the front yard! Daddy, they dug a hole! Daddy, come and see. Daddy, they are putting a stick in the hole!"

I reached behind me to flush and discovered there was something wrong with the toilet. Then when I went to turn on the water to wash my hands, all I heard was gurgling air passing through the pipes. As I was standing there in that tiny half bathroom, it dawned on me that my water was being cut off because I was 90 days late—it was not the first time.

As I stood there with no water to wash my hands or flush, the stench just permeated every cell of my body. I'm talking about the stench of my life—the stench of imminent foreclosure; the stench of me, Mr. Big Bad Business Owner, who could not even pay the water bill on time. The stench of my feeling depressed and sorry for myself combined with my half-assed fathering and half-assed husbandry was choking me.

I mean, I won all blue ribbons at field day in third grade. I was an 11-year-old successful *GRIT* newspaper boy. I was a starting linebacker in a national championship game. I am a United States Marine. I was selected for the elite Yankee White program. I even guarded President Reagan— what would the Gipper say about this marine now? Yet still, here I was immerced in the stench of my average, broke, disappointing life.

So I looked deep into the eyes reflected in the mirror, and in a moment of complete misery, embarrassment, frustration, and disappointment, I just started to scream. There were no words; it was just a scream of utter disgust. My soul had had enough and could not take another moment of this life.

I was everything I never wanted to be.

The front that I had it all together was just a mirage—smoke and mirrors. My fairy tale life wasn't *Beauty and the Beast*. At my house the fairy tale was "Beauty and the Least."

When I tried to flush that toilet and my stench didn't go anywhere, it was a metaphor for my life. I knew I had to do something to wake myself up. Otherwise, I wasn't going to lose just my house, but I was going to lose myself, my business, and the love of my family. My wife had been following behind me, picking up the broken pieces for so long. Any other human would have left me to die in the desert of disappointment and saved themselves.

The life I had dreamed up all those years ago was fractured and bleeding out, about to flatline. I could not shake the grip of failure. It felt like I was just a collection of disappointments and empty promises; the warrior marine I used to be was missing in action.

Then at the end of that deafening scream of my soul, the fog lifted. The eyes of my soul became clear, and an awareness rose up from deep inside me. This new, but familiar, awareness lit a fire in me that had not burned for 16 years.

Our entire lives we are told that failure is bad—failure is for failures, they say. So I was determined to fight failure from a young age. I saw myself as a champion, a thoroughbred that never failed. My view of failure was tainted and skewed.

In that awakening moment, in that tiny half bathroom, failure lost all its power over me. I stopped fighting failure. I evolved my relationship with failure.

The skewed thinking I had adopted was that failing meant you were a failure. So when failure showed up in my life, I resisted it. I fought with it like Jacob did with the angel. Yet this fight was always won by failure, and I ended up with my face in the mud of disappointment, with failure's boot on the back of my neck every single time.

Is this where you are right now? Is your face down in the mud pit of disappointment? Does failure have its boot pressing down on the back of your neck? Have you given up on yourself? Have you given up on those dreams that kept you up late into the night with anticipation and excitement? Have you surrendered to failure and disappointment? Are you waving the white flag, even though you have so many promising days left in your life? Are you scrolling and bingeing to numb the scream of your soul?

When I broke the code on failure and success, I was finally able to free myself from the chains of disappointment; I was able to step out of the shackles of frustration. I became free of the prison that failure had locked me in for over 16 years.

I thought there was something wrong with me. Do you think there is something wrong with you? Do you look in the mirror and ask, "What's wrong with me?" or "Why can't I shake this?"

IT'S NOT YOUR FAULT!!!

It's faulty programming. Our entire lives we are taught that failure is bad. Get an F in school and "Oh my goodness, wait until your father sees this" or "What is grandma going to say about this F?" After all, F stands for failure.

If you lose your job, everybody will shun you and shake their head. Or God forbid you lose your house—you'll have the whole neighborhood driving by slowly to watch you move out, judgment thick in the streets.

If you fail at marriage, the people at church and in your family all pick sides. It might feel like you've been branded with a scarlet letter—suddenly you're uninvited and unwelcome.

We are told that failure is bad our entire lives. We are repeatedly warned to "Be careful," "Play it safe," or "Be realistic." And above all, "Don't get your hopes up."

As I broke the code on failure, my dreams became real; money became attainable, a successful business was achievable, my marriage blossomed, and my kids wanted to be around me.

LIFE DIDN'T CHANGE; I CHANGED!!!

The struggles are the same, obstacles still happen, but it doesn't have me. I HAVE IT!!!

As the revolution was happening to me, a formula evolved. I started sharing that formula with people, and they started to manifest results that had eluded them for years.

Chris owned his business for three years when he hired me as his success coach. Chris is an intelligent college graduate who is also a parent and an athlete. But the first three years of his business were a struggle. As we started working together, Chris took my success formula and became laser focused. We spoke once a month, and I would send him texts. In 90 days he went from $20,000 in his best month in the winter (his busy time) to $49,000 in July (the slowest time of the year for his business). I am so proud of Chris. He was able to transform his life in many ways as a father, husband, and business owner because this success formula works.

This is not a weight-loss system, yet when applied to weight loss, you will lose weight.

Stacie was out of shape. She was tired all the time, her back hurt, and her knees hurt. She had been overweight most her life, and after the birth of her son, her struggle with weight only became harder. She was in a prison of failure and disappointment; it seemed hopeless. When she connected with me about this struggle, I shared what I had learned, and she started to apply it to her life. It didn't happen overnight, but as Stacie changed how she viewed herself and failure, she evolved back into her true self. She loved dancing and music. She discovered Zumba so I encouraged her to become certified to teach Zumba. She was ready with a list of excuses as to why she couldn't become a Zumba teacher: I don't have the money. They are all skinny and sleek . . . After she finished her litany of protests, she decided to take the risk, and it was a transformative moment for her.

Stacie's first revelation was that Zumba teachers are all shapes and sizes. When she first began teaching, her class consisted of just her mom and one friend. Then two more people joined. Then that multiplied into 10 people. And now every Tuesday and Thursday, 30-plus people show up to her class. Stacie has become so active that she now does obstacle course racing with her son, and she was even in a parade with her crew, doing Zumba. I am so proud of her complete transformation.

This is Stacie on an obstacle in a Tough Mudder.

I am writing this book because there are things that have happened in my life that have wounded me. I've carried them around for the majority of my life. My dream in writing this book is to help you release whatever painful events that have happened in your life that are holding you back from achieving your goals.

Failure has been holding you hostage for too long. My goal in writing this book is to help you break through whatever is stopping you from going for the BIG. I will break you out of the prison of failure. This book will set you free to go for the big and live your dream life.

I am putting my heart and my soul in words and offering it to you because I want to share what helped me transform my destiny.

Based on my past, I should be divorced. I should be struggling financially and emotionally. Through applying the lessons I've learned, I've become a great husband, a fabulous father, and a successful business owner in the top 1 percent of the income bracket. I'm proud of all of that.

My lifelong desire and passion has been to influence others and help them go for the BIG. I am here to help you identify and overcome whatever is stopping you from achieving your goals. I know what it feels like to be stuck, and I believe I've had the experiences I've had to help you get unstuck.

If achieving success feels like trying to catch a fish with your bare hands, or if getting to the next level feels impossible, then this book will help you break through.

I have worked with many CEOs, executives, and entrepreneurs in a variety of businesses, and I've helped them break through to the next level. I started working with one of my clients right after he was released from jail. His expertise was in the construction business, and within two years I helped him generate $2.4 million in revenue.

Art, another one of my clients, is the CEO of a restoration company, and I helped him save $100,000 a year in marketing.

Here is a link to see a video of Art Evans:

https://www.youtube.com/watch?v=3AqOkYovEOE&t=11s&lIst=PLZ cZPEZmj-UTvtDf6HD-eueKhOWxX_QjC&Index=67

I am an expert in helping people go for the BIG and break through to the next level in their lives and careers.

If you dedicate yourself to this book, you will break through; you will achieve your BIG!

CHAPTER ONE

Playing It Small Is Selfish

You are here on the planet to let your light shine. You are here to be epic and extraordinary. For different people, and at different times, being epic and extraordinary will mean different things. For the man that just lost his family in a tragic accident, getting out of bed and getting a cup of coffee might be a Herculean task. The next day his epic might be getting a cup of coffee and sitting out on the porch for an hour. The day after that, letting his light shine might be walking down the street.

For the business owner, letting their light shine may be getting health benefits for all your staff.

The entrepreneur that daily goes out and gets three noes to find a yes is shining brightly.

For the preacher, letting their light shine may be having a service of worship with a full live band on Saturday nights.

I'm using these examples because I want you to understand that when I say go for the BIG, I mean to make progress. Breakthrough to the next level from where you are right now. Once we arrive there, we'll attack the next BIG and then the next BIG. Going for the BIG is not a final destination. Going for the BIG is a beautiful, engaging process. Letting your light shine is a result of continuously going for the BIG.

Playing it small is selfish, playing it small is not natural for you, and it doesn't serve anybody else.

Inside of you is the desire to go for the BIG. The opposite of that desire is playing it small. It is an intense and eternal battle. Often we don't even realize that we are playing it small. We don't recognize the infinite ways we give in to the numbing voice that lulls us into retreating from our dreams. When we binge on entire seasons of TV shows on Netflix or scroll social media for hours at a time, we are numbing ourselves. When we eat an entire cake in one sitting or do drugs, smoke, or drink to excess, we are attempting to escape from going for our BIG. We are trying to mute the scream of our soul.

When you play it small and refuse to let your light shine, you have your eyes on three people: me, myself, and I.

When you play it small you're worried about failing; you're concerned about rejection or being uncomfortable. Ultimately, you're not sure if you're good enough, so you play it small and save yourself the risk of failing.

Recently I was in Tennessee, and I visited an underground lake. It was about 1,200 feet underground, and we were in a glass-bottom boat on this underground lake, so we could see the fish in the water. The tour guide shared that all the fish in the lake were blind because there is zero light down there. It was partially lit so we could see, but the natural habitat is complete darkness.

I asked what would happen if a human were down there, and the tour guide told me that within two weeks of absolute darkness, the human eye would go blind. When I heard that I thought about how selfish we are when we don't let our light shine.

There are people in our lives living in complete darkness. When we selfishly play small and don't let our light shine, we are allowing those

10

people to go blind. They are in absolute darkness when we don't go for the BIG.

You are someone's only light. There are people only you can save.

When you play it small everyone around you loses; yet when you let your light shine, you light the way for everyone around you. When you let your light shine, you give everyone around you permission to let their light shine. Think how much brighter the world will be once you are fully shining your light!

Now, I'm not saying that letting your light shine is easy. It's a struggle, and of course, there will be times when you won't succeed. When you play it small, you're afraid of failure, of rejection, and ultimately of success.

Wake up. Playing it small costs the same as letting your light shine.

When you play it small, you're going to feel rejection and failure as well because you're not even going for your dream, so of course, you feel like a failure. When you let your light shine, you're taking a risk. You will fail. You will be rejected. However, you will also succeed.

When you call that client that you've been scared to call, sure, they can say no. When you raise your prices to better reflect the value of your services, you might lose customers. But when you don't call that customer, you still don't have them. You lost them simply by not taking action. When you don't raise your prices, you cost yourself time that you could have been spending with your family.

If you have a hundred customers and you raise your prices by 50 percent, and you lose half your customers, what did you gain? You earned time. You're making the same amount of money in half the amount of time.

When I say take a risk, when I say let your light shine, I'm talking about your going to the next level. I want you to know that it's going to cost you the same whether you let your light shine or you play it small. Rejection and failure are happening if you play it small simply because you're not in your natural state of shining. You were created to shine.

The people you are meant to inspire are in utter darkness when you play it small. They are lost; they don't know what to do. Imagine you're going for the BIG and one of your employees can put their child through college. Would that be worth the risk that you'd have to take to let your light shine?

Imagine that you sign that customer you were scared of calling and deliver excellent service to them and now they're able to grow their business. You started that chain reaction because you took a risk by calling them. That risk resulted in everyone winning. That's why playing it small is selfish.

If you want to let your light shine, find a coach and be open to being coached.

Stacie went from playing it small and being afraid to follow her passion, to inspiring other people to get in shape. It is amazing the influence that she has on her audience. She has been able to help people lower their blood pressure, get off diabetes medicine, and just be healthier and sexier overall. We continued to work together, and now she's so excited about her life and her success. I'm excited too, and I encourage her to set the next goal.

Remember, going for the BIG is progressive. Letting your light shine is a lifetime pursuit.

Her next challenge was to teach a cardio class. Of course, her fears shouted, "I can't teach cardio. I'm just getting Zumba right!" I pointed out how far she'd already come. In addition to her Zumba following, she was running on the treadmill, doing the rowing machine, and doing ball slams—those were BIG achievements based on where she began. She was still a little insecure that her body wasn't as tight as some of the instructors that she was comparing herself to, but she overcame those fears. She started teaching cardio because she knew she had nothing to lose by going for it, and what she could gain was immeasurable.

She had 10 people attend her first cardio class, and they loved it! Now she teaches a cardio blast twice a week to a diverse class that includes men, women, and children. Sometimes she teaches in the park, and sometimes it's inside of the gym. She enjoys creating evolving lesson plans, so it's new and enjoyable for everyone. She incorporates everything from flipping tires to jumping rope, so it's never the same class twice. She's just growing and growing and becoming happier and happier. It started with her willingness to override her doubts and fears. The result of her taking that personal risk changed her life and the lives of hundreds of her students. In fact, she was probably even more inspiring because she didn't have the traditional fitness teacher body.

When you let your light shine, someone's going to come out of the darkness and begin to see because you took a risk and allowed your light to shine.

Letting your light shine is what you were designed to do. It is in your DNA. It is actually your natural state of being. There will be some people who might be jealous when you let your light shine. Perhaps your brightness shines a light on their insecurities and how they are not going for their dreams. However, you never need to apologize for being a hero. You do not need to apologize for letting your light shine and being amazing.

At this point you might be saying, "But Michael, I did it. I let my light shine, and I completely failed. My friends all laughed at me, and I was totally embarrassed. I will never do that again. NEVER!!!"

First, notice how many times me, myself, and I show up in this statement:

- *I* failed
- *My* friends
- *I* was
- *I* will

This statement is all about me, myself, and I. Who was inspired by you? What did you learn? How are you better, smarter, stronger from shining bright?

Second, "I will never do that again. NEVER!" Really? Have you ever been in a car accident or knew someone that was? Have you been in a car since that accident? Why? How could you get back in a car after total, utter failure? See my point? If you have failed after shining bright and going for the BIG, that does not in any way give you permission to not shine more or not go for the big again.

If Stacie stopped after two people showed up to her first class, 60 people a week would have lost out on an opportunity to move and dance and have a great time.

Now you might be saying "Michael, I hear you and I get it, but I can't go for the BIG right now. The kids are in school. I just got married. I don't have the money. [Blah, blah, blah . . .]" That's more me, myself, and I. You can only shine right now. You cannot shine into the future. You cannot shine into the past. Now as you are this moment is all you have.

I have a friend. She's only 47 years old. Her life flashed before her. One minute, she's doing fine. The next minute she's in the hospital, talking to doctors about how to survive and recover from this at 47. I have another friend that had a massive heart attack. He's 36, and he has an electric battery on his hip, and the strap goes over his shoulder, and that electric battery is pumping his heart, and he is on the list to get a heart transplant at 36.

The only time you can shine your light is right now. It needs to be a sense of urgency. There are people that only you can reach. Remember that. Make it a requirement; let your light shine, because there are people that only you can reach. You are the only light that's going to reach them, save them, and help them start to shine.

Remember, playing it small is not safe, and it inspires no one. I want you to SHINE SO BRIGHT THE SUN IS JEALOUS!

https://www.themichaelbottsexperience.com/
http://l.ead.me/bavy8w

CHAPTER TWO

Failure Is Your Friend

How can failure be your friend? You've been thinking failure is bad your whole life. Actually, that hasn't been the case your entire life. When we were babies, failure wasn't bad. When you were learning to walk, people cheered even when you were falling. As a toddler you never once turned down mashed peas as you sat in the high chair because of the stress caused by your failure to master walking. Not once did you lay awake at night, pushing Mama's milk away because you had failed at walking all day. Nope, you just failed and failed and failed and failed until finally, after many scrapes and bruises, you began to take one baby step at a time. As you started growing up, gradually you became programmed to see failure as a bad thing.

Here's the good news: FAILURE IS YOUR FRIEND. How in the world could you go for the BIG if failure is not your best friend? Going for the BIG is really about falling in love with failing.

The truth is that you have failed your whole life, and still, here you are reading this book. You still possess limitless opportunities. Think about your last BIG failure. How long did you sulk? Are you still moping around? Be honest. How big a deal was it? Even if you lost your house, which is more common these days, so what? You are not a failure; you merely experienced a failure. You went for the BIG of owning a home, and you failed. Did you die? If you're reading this, you didn't die. Has anyone on the planet ever lost their house, and been able to buy another house, and paid it off? Of course, they have.

Here's something I always tell myself: what one man can do, another man can do. Failure is just part of going for the BIG, just like getting wet is part of going swimming. When you go for the BIG, it's impossible for you not to fail.

I don't use *impossible* loosely, because I'm not a fan of the word impossible, but I want you to understand that failure is an integral part of the complete process of going for the BIG.

If you settle for average and continue to play it small, that is failure. If you go for the BIG, there's going to be failure.

Here's a newsflash: you cannot avoid failure. If you're alive on the planet, you cannot prevent failure.

In reality, you should be proud of yourself when you fail. This is a transformative switch in thinking. However, we can switch it in one second. Just right now, give yourself permission to embrace failure. Every time failure shows up I just want you to give it a loving kiss.

Here is what I want you to understand: failure and success are twins, and you have to date one in order to date the other. You have to date failure if you want to date success. You have to kiss failure. You have to take failure to dinner and buy it flowers. Once you fall in love with failure, then success is going to get jealous and chase you down. Success will be in relentless pursuit of you, and the same way you would plan for a date, you need to have a fail plan.

Perhaps you think that sounds ridiculous—making a plan to fail—but that's not what I said. Your plan is to succeed, but I need you to have a plan for when failure shows up.

It used to be that when I failed I would sulk around. I wouldn't be productive; in short, I was a train wreck. However, what I've discovered is that I'm in charge of failure; it is not in charge of me. I get to decide how long I'm going to sulk.

Perhaps I'll allow it two hours. That means that for two hours I'm going to flail around, eat chocolate pudding, and feel sorry for myself. I'm going to watch a movie, and cry, and sulk around. It's funny because once I realize that I'm in charge of it, I can turn it off. I can stop whenever I want.

If you and I are both going for the same goal, and we both miss it, and you recover in five minutes, but it takes me a year to recover, that doesn't mean I loved the goal more or that it was more important to me. It means I felt sorry for myself longer. It means my relationship with failure is immature, and yours is evolved and mature.

If you recover from your failure right away, that doesn't mean you didn't value the goal enough. It means you've trained yourself to recover rapidly.

When I coach athletes, they already know that they are never going to play a perfect game. They have already learned to train their brains to recover rapidly. They cannot afford to sulk in the middle of game. When they get it wrong, they need to recover swiftly and keep moving.

The same lesson applies to entrepreneurs. If they spend time sulking and moping when something goes wrong, they'll end up missing other clients. Every minute that I feel sorry for myself is one less person that's inspired and motivated to go for the BIG. Once I focus on serving those people, it's a little easier to get out of the rut of feeling sorry for myself.

Once you become aware that you are in control, you can have some fun with it. What if you ask yourself some questions like "What is funny about this fail?" You know that once you're sitting around, telling your friends about it that you're going to laugh at it. Why can't you just laugh about it today? Go on, call the girls over, break out the wine, and just have a party about it. Or meet the boys at happy hour and open with your epic fail. Simply embrace the failure.

Sit down at the feet of failure, and look at it like it were Yoda, and ask, "What is the lesson I need to learn from this?" Failure will answer.

You know that each failure you've experienced has taught you a great lesson if you allowed it. Of course, it's your choice to shut yourself off from learning. You can feel sorry for yourself and be mad at it. You can fight failure all you want. You can complain that it's not fair (we will deal with this in a few pages), and that might be true. However, you won't move forward in your own life if you do that, nor will you inspire others.

Remember, you are the most powerful force on the planet. YOU ARE THE MOST POWERFUL FORCE ON THE PLANET!!! You can take another shot at your goal immediately. You can do it smarter, better, stronger, or you can wait a year and take another shot. It's totally up to you.

Here's the formula for recovering from failure:

1. *Forgive yourself*—We are hardest on ourselves. If we treated anyone else the way we treat ourselves after a failure, it would be considered assault. I am an expert at feeling bad for feeling bad; it is just ridiculous. Feeling bad for feeling bad is an absolute spiral into depression and disappointment. It's a total waste. Give yourself permission to feel bad and recover.

2. *Ask forgiveness if you failed others*—If you had employees that were counting on payroll and you didn't make it, you need to talk to

them and let them know what happened. If you didn't deliver for a client, don't offer excuses. Just take full responsibility and ask for another chance to redeem yourself.

3. *Learn*—The whole purpose of failure is to learn. Once you've learned the lesson, you can go again faster, stronger, and better.

4. *Go again*—If you go again right away, you have more power. The longer you wait, the heavier the failure feels.

When my son Noah was around 6 years old, we went horseback riding and he saw his mom get bucked off of her horse and suffer a hard landing. It shook him up. He was scared, but we took him right back out and got him back on the horse again within the next few days. We didn't let it build up into a situation where he became afraid of horses. Noah has the beautiful ability to face his fears head on. He literally got right back on the horse!

get help—You need to have an expert or a mentor. It's imperative. Don't just try to do it on your own. You are enough, but why not have some help?

Think of the people who have succeeded in their chosen endeavor. All of them have had a coach or a teacher. Look at Michael Jordan, Tiger Woods, LeBron James—all athletes of note have coaches and trainers that have urged them to greatness.

Even super coach Tony Robbins had a mentor and a coach. There are people out there that have walked through the minefield and survived. Let's walk along the path they've forged and expand it.

When you choose your experts, make sure they're people who are going to encourage you and lift you up. Qualify your experts.

If you're trying to stay married, you shouldn't ask Aunt Julie for marriage advice if she's on her twelfth divorce. Apparently, Aunt Julie doesn't know how to stay married; she knows how to get divorced. If you want to lose weight, you probably shouldn't ask someone that hasn't lost weight. If you want to own a successful business, I would say your expert should be someone that's owned a successful business.

Please understand that everyone who has achieved success has experienced failure. The point is they overcame the failure and created a victory. That's the type of person I would choose as my expert.

You're closer than you think—Each failure is an opportunity to go again, smarter, better, and stronger. Embrace the failure as proof of advancement. Your next time at bat could result in a grand slam.

When Thomas Edison was inventing the light bulb, he said, "I have not failed. I have just found 10,000 ways that won't work." Ten thousand fails? Wow, we would still be using candles if it were up to me.

Thomas Edison also said, "Our greatest weakness lies in giving up. The most certain way to succeed is always to just try one more time."

One more time. How hard would it be to quit if you knew the next sales conversation was an absolute yes? Failure is a stairway to success. Every time you experience a failure, you have also taken one step closer to success, and you've gained that much more wisdom and strength along the way.

FEAR OF FAILURE

For some people, fear of failure is the only obstacle to success. If you are haunted by the fear of failure, you cannot go for the BIG. I believe that you picked up this book up because you're ready to overcome that fear. You want to go for the BIG in your life, and this book is your roadmap.

At 13 years old, my son Elijah would grab a snow shovel and trek out into two feet of snow and knock on doors, offering his shoveling services.

The fear of failure was not even on his radar. He knew no after no meant a yes was getting closer.

This is your moment. Once you genuinely understand that failure is truly your friend, then the fear dissipates. Going for the BIG is just a process of overcoming a string of failures and learning from each one. My advice is to do it as a sprint, knowing that you will break the tape of success at the end of the race.

However, if you're associating with people that belittle you or bring you down when you encounter a failure, then you need a new crowd.

Surround yourself with people who encourage you to go again. The next time you fail, I want you to share it with your 10 closest friends and watch their reactions. The friends who support you and encourage you to keep trying are the ones that you need to keep close. The friends that say things like "I told you not to try" are the people you don't need to share your failures or your successes with. You need to make sure you're associating with people that understand that failure is part of the process of achievement. "Show me your friends, and I'll show you your future."

TRYING TO AVOID FAILURE IS FAILURE

By avoiding failure, you are still failing! I want you to think about that for a moment. As you go for the BIG, you're going to fail. It's part of the program. However, when you don't go for the BIG, you are failing 100 percent.

If you're breathing, there's going to be failure in your life, so why not go for what you really want? Even If you fail epically, you can live with no regrets.

As my daughter Mikayla entered high school, she had the goal of becoming a triathlete, meaning she'd play three different sports each school year—freshman, sophomore, junior, and senior years.

Her freshman year she played basketball and softball, and she made the cheerleading squad. Her sophomore year she continued with cheerleading, which had become a passion; she made the JV basketball team; and she added lacrosse. So she's reached her goal two years in a row with two years to go.

As a sophomore she didn't feel she was getting enough play on the basketball team, so she went to speak with her coach. The coach told her to step up her game, which hurt, but she continued working hard on the team.

Now it's junior year, and she made the lacrosse team, and she's still a cheerleader, but she wasn't chosen for the basketball team. This really hurt. Not only was she fond of the coach, but she was sad that she wouldn't be playing alongside all the friends she'd made on the team over the last two years.

I was there in the lobby as she left the basketball tryouts having just learned that she would no longer be on the team. She was trying to hold back her tears so everyone wouldn't see her crying, and the first thing I said to her was "Okay, what's plan B? What can we do to make sure you still reach your determination to play three sports per year?" This is not what she wanted to hear at this time. She was still dealing with the sting of failure and disappointment.

However, the very next day (notice she gave herself a time limit to sulk and recover) she decided to talk to the track coach about trying out for that team, and she ended up being chosen to be a shot putter.

She worked at it and became the second-best shot putter in the school and placed ninth at a regional conference. So she was able to still achieve her triathlete goal.

Mikayla transformed her setback into a setup for a comeback!

Also, an interesting note about the cheerleading team is that she had made the JV team as a sophomore, but she really wanted to be on the varsity team. Then a few days after tryouts, the cheerleading coach sent out a mass text saying they were having another varsity tryout because someone had to step down, so they had one more slot available.

Mikayla jumped at the chance to try again for varsity, and when she arrived at the tryout, she was the only one there, so guess who got that spot? She did! My dad always used to say that showing up is half the battle. That year she led her cheer squad to a conference championship.

I want you to know that it's possible for you to sprint through the failure, jumping each hurdle as they arise. Sulking and grieving doesn't prove how much you wanted it. Your goal is to rapidly recover from the failure and go again. Once you embrace failure, success will be in hot pursuit. Use the plan that I put in this chapter to help you recover from failure rapidly. Every failure is a step closer to a success.

https://www.themichaelbottsexperience.com/
http://l.ead.me/bavy8w

CHAPTER THREE

Epic Quantum Leaps of Action

Most of our lives we've been warned to be careful, to be realistic, to aim a little bit lower, and to not get our hopes up. We are reminded with statistics that we don't have a chance—for example, people love to tell entrepreneurs that eight out of 10 businesses fail. We've been programmed to play it small or to not play at all.

Yet the truth of us, what's in our DNA, underneath all the pain, fear, and doubt, is a sleeping giant. You possess a hundred-pound gorilla of action waiting to be awakened and to take epic quantum leaps of action.

No one really has a deep desire to play it small. Playing it small is not something to fight toward. Playing it small does not make you excited to get out of bed in the morning. We all truly want whatever our version of BIG looks like. The way to achieve our version of BIG is to take epic quantum leaps of action. What does all of that mean? Let's break it down:

The definition of *epic* is "very great, large, and unusually difficult; impressive."

Quantum leap is defined as "an abrupt, large, decisive increase."

Action means "an act of will or a thing that is done."

Put together, an *epic quantum leap of action* is "an impressive abrupt increase of action of will to get a thing done."

Notice, the title of this chapter isn't "Epic Quantum Leaps of Results." The title is "Epic Quantum Leaps of Action" because action is within our control. If we take epic quantum leaps of action, success and failure will absolutely follow us. If instead of taking action we watch an entire season of *Grey's Anatomy*, then our results will reflect that choice. However, if we stay tuned into our goal and work toward it from sunup to sundown, then those results will also be reflected as well.

It is also important to note the difference between action and results. Action is something that I can control. I wake up in the morning, I have a list of what I'm going for, and I take action. Results are what come out of taking that action. We need to embrace action instead of embracing the results. Our action will absolutely influence the results, but when we focus on the results, this will influence our action.

Love that you went for a walk (ACTION) as opposed to loving that you lost a pound or hating that you didn't lose a pound (RESULT). Love that you went and had a sales conversation with five potential clients (ACTION) as opposed to loving that you made a sale or hating that you didn't make a sale (RESULT). Fall in love with your amazing ability to continually take epic quantum leaps of action.

OUR OLD PROGRAMMING

Because of our early programming, we may shy away from taking epic quantum leaps of action. You may be a little scared right now. Or your inner voice might be saying, "This sounds like a lot of work, and I'm lazy. My whole life my family told me that I was lazy."

This is the average you (am I enough?) threatened by this new train of thought. The average you (am I enough?) wants to sit on the couch and watch an entire season of *One Tree Hill*. The average you (am I enough?) wants to eat hamburgers and drink sodas. The average you (am I enough?) wants to just settle for your current income level and the lifestyle that it affords. The average you (am I enough?) wants to play it safe and maybe not go to the next relationship, because you could get hurt. The average you (am I enough?) is threatened because it knows its days are numbered.

Warning: we are going to choke the average you. We need to drown the average you in a pool of your taking epic quantum leaps of action. The average you has to go because it is not really who you are.

HAVE YOU MET YOU?

I'm not sure that you know how powerful you are. You have been underestimating yourself. For so long, you have believed the delusion that you're average. You have fallen under the spell of "am I enough?" and "I can't." You have embraced the belief that you're not special. That's an easy and comfortable place to be, and many people live in that land their entire lives. But I am here to help you move out, because actually, you're amazing, and I can't let you live in the land of average any longer.

The person who picked up this book cannot live in the "I can't," "It's not fair," or "It's not my fault" blame-game zone. So go ahead and release any thoughts like this that are holding you back.

You are dynamic. You are a living, talking miracle, and your DNA is impregnated with greatness. You are brilliant. You are limitless. Think about all you have been through to be here alive, breathing, reading this book. You survived other humans raising you, you survived all the bacteria and viruses, and you survived siblings.

You might still be afraid of taking epic quantum leaps of action, and that's okay. You are allowed to take baby steps, since ultimately, slow motion is better than no motion. However, it is my desire to inspire you to take epic quantum leaps of action because that is the true you. Once you believe in your greatness and decide to truly go for the BIG, you will be leaping toward fulfilling your mission, not taking baby steps. When you were just a toddler, you looked up the ladder of the big slide with total confidence and started to climb. You didn't have doubt or fear. You were full of the pure certainty of "I AM ENOUGH." That's the true you before life sucked you under and filled your lungs full of limiting beliefs.

This is gonna ruffle some feathers.

There isn't a shortage of energy. There isn't a shortage of water. There isn't a shortage of food, of love, of kindness and generosity. There is only one shortage on this planet. The only shortage on this planet is of humans that will take epic quantum leaps of action. I mean, think about it. Every solution to every problem that the human race has faced and solved has come out of a human, humans taking epic quantum leaps of action.

Let's just take some examples.

Problem: the moon is out there. Solution? Man on the moon. Some people took epic quantum leaps of action, and they put a man on the moon.

Problem: it takes months to cross the United States. Solution? The Transcontinental Railroad. It took epic quantum leaps of action to solve that problem and to take that risk and to go for that BIG.

Problem: we can't fly. Solution? The Wright Brothers' taking flight. It is an amazing story of what the Wright Brothers went through to achieve motorized flight. And they had many rejections and many struggles. But they were taking epic quantum leaps of action to get to their goal.

This is one of my favorites. Problem: The polio virus was paralyzing thousands of kids a day. Every day, thousands of kids were getting the polio virus and becoming paralyzed. Solution? The polio vaccine. Distributing across the world and 99 percent eradication of the polio virus. That is an epic quantum leap of action. And what followed it? An epic quantum leap result. So let's make sure we're clear: results will follow if you take these epic quantum leaps of action.

The only thing between your barely paying your bills and your making a boatload of money is an epic quantum leap of action. From you being lonely and sad to you feeling lovingly fulfilled is an epic quantum leap of action. Clean drinking water for the whole planet is simply humans taking epic quantum leaps of action. That's the only thing. And I promise you, baby steps will work. But know this—you were built for epic quantum leaps of action. That is your destiny. That is what you were built for.

There's a plant called the Chinese bamboo tree. In the first year you don't see any results, In fact, you don't see any results for four years. Then after five years of watering, fertilizing, and hoping for growth, you start wondering if you've been wasting your time, when finally a tiny sprout pops up. It's tiny, but after all this time at least it's something you can latch your hope and belief onto. Then in the next six short weeks the Chinese bamboo tree grows 90 feet. That is equal to one inch of growth an hour. You have to keep the faith when doubt and fear and limiting beliefs are surrounding you. Trust that all of your epic quantum leaps of action will pay off.

Why shouldn't they pay off? Why not you, and why not now? Really, what do you have to lose? What's the worst that could happen? You already don't have what you want. It's out there, away from you. So you can't lose what you already don't have.

You may be able to measure "what's the worst that can happen?"

For example, if I call this customer, they could say no. Sure. However, you cannot measure what's the best that could happen. Maybe you'll call them, they'll say yes and refer you to 10 of their associates, and on we go!!!

Sometimes you can measure your potential losses, but what you have to gain is infinite. Start taking epic quantum leaps of action.

If you were guaranteed success, what would be your goal? How high would you leap? I want you to write that down right now.

Get out some paper and a pen and write it down!

Now I want you to do it. Put the book down now, and take that leap. I bet you're scared right now. You're supposed to be afraid and uncomfortable right now. The average you is screaming, and hollering, and kicking like its life depends on it, because it does. By taking that leap, you are transforming from average you into epic you.

You have a choice right now. Are you going to listen to the average you? Are you going to listen to the old programming that says, "You're lazy. You can't do this. Nobody wants you. You are not enough"? Or are you going to jump in with me and take this epic quantum leap?

Right now, overcome the fear, doubt, and worry of being rejected; take that leap right now. Why not you? Why not now? You have everything to gain. Leap right now.

You're probably saying, "Wait a minute. We're getting a little carried away here. I wrote it down. That's about as close to the edge as I want to get today. I'm on the edge of the chair, but I don't want to actually get up out of the recliner of average." That's just fear talking.

When you first rode a bike, you were scared, but you didn't let it stop you, because you knew, deep down in your heart, you were supposed to be able to ride a bike. Right now you're scared and you're uncomfortable. Take this epic quantum leap of action. Do it now. Now is the only time.

You know deep down you are supposed to do this right now. I want you to trust your inner voice. It has never lied to you, and it has never been wrong.

I bet you've been putting things off until tomorrow your whole life. Perhaps you're waiting for something to be perfect. Let me tell you when the ideal time is: now.

As much as you need oxygen, you need to take this epic quantum leap of action. Whatever it is, you need to do it. Sprint into the fear, attack the doubt, and explode the limiting belief. Now is the time for you to get it done. Take an epic quantum leap of action.

Action will silence fear all day long!

As my 14 year old son Caleb and i sit in our car in a dark parking lot tears coming down his face reflect the parking lot lights. inside the gym a team tryout/practice is about to start that he has been invited to. Now this kid is the poster child for work ethic i have dropped him and his brother Noah at the basketball court at noon and picked them up at 9pm he loves basketball and he works hard at it. Fear had snuck in, doubt had grabbed him in a choke hold. he was not sure he wanted to go in and risk failing. We sat there talking about what was the worst that could happen "not make the team" i said your already not on the team. He looked at me and kind of chuckles. he pulls himself together gathers his gear and reaches for the door handle then a short pause, he takes a deep breath and pulls the handle and pushes the door open. As he walks into that gym he discovered a truth "Action will silence fear".

https://www.themichaelbottsexperience.com/
http://l.ead.me/bavy8w

CHAPTER FOUR

Falling Down Is Allowed; Getting Up Is Required

Why do salmon swim upstream? Why do they leave the safety of the ocean, where they have plenty of food and the threats of death are minimal, to answer the call to swim upstream?

The river is a deadly gauntlet of threats. They have to battle their way up shallow, rocky riverbeds. They have to escape bears waiting to crush them with their powerful jaws and outmaneuver the eagles swooping in to sink their talons into their backs. They battle all of this just to answer the call inside of them.

We are like the salmon in this way. We have a mysterious call, the cry of our soul to do something epic—to go for the BIG. Going for the BIG is just like battling our way up the mouth of the river lined with a gauntlet of obstacles waiting to pounce on our dream.

The idea of facing all of those obstacles might make you really want to stay cozy in that recliner of average, but if you don't heed the call to swim up upstream, to go for the BIG, you will die.

Okay, Michael, you went off the deep end now. Will I die? Really? You're saying if I don't go for the big, I'm going to die?

Yes, the salmon is built to swim upstream. That's its destiny. When a salmon doesn't swim upstream, it dies. You are built to go for the big. That is your destiny. When you settle for the average life, you begin to die.

See, you cannot ignore the cry of your soul. What will you do to mute that cry? Eat yourself to death? Drink yourself to death? Relationship yourself to death? Work yourself to death? Spend yourself to death? Somehow, you have to try and mute the cry of your soul, the cry to go for the BIG.

In an attempt to mute your screaming soul, you get a bunch of distractions, like eating, drinking, smoking, going from relationship to relationship, shopping, being negative, complaining, and blaming everyone. Your arteries start to clog. Your back begins to hurt. You gain excess weight. You become negative and sarcastic about everything. You pick fights with the ones you love or just shut yourself off from them completely.

All this in an attempt to numb the cry of your soul. So yes, not answering the cry of your soul ends in a death of regret.

This is life or death. If you don't go for the BIG, you'll die. I am on a mission to reveal the epic, relentless, limitless you. This is your life. Wake up! Wake up out of the slumber of average and go for the BIG.

I have a mantra for you. This mantra has saved my marriage, my business, and my life a multitude of times. Here it is. Sit up in your seat. Pay attention. Your life will never be the same.

"Falling down is allowed; getting up is required."

Just take a moment and say it out loud. Now, stand up and do your best superhero pose, and say it with passion and energy. How does that feel?

If you embrace the truth of this beautiful mantra, you can go for the BIG with confidence and certainty. You were born with this mantra imprinted on your DNA, and I can prove it.

AM I ENOUGH?

You were born into a state of believing "I AM ENOUGH." You had no fear, no doubt, and no question of "am I enough?" You were full of confidence and determination. As you tried to crawl and then walk, you failed thousands of times before you got it right, but never, not once, did you stress about walking. You didn't turn down your mashed peas and carrots because you were so worried about failing to walk. Not once did you push away a warm bottle of Mama's milk because you were busy stressing out about how many times you failed at walking. You just ate those mashed peas and drank Mama's milk and slept like a baby because on your DNA is imprinted "falling down is allowed; getting up is required."

Swimming upstream is hard. It's dangerous. Going for the big is hard and dangerous, but so is learning to walk. You didn't focus on the danger or how hard it was. You just kept at it because you knew, deep down in your DNA, that falling down was allowed and getting up was required. You've seen others do it, so you knew it could be done.

As you learned to walk, every fall, scrape, and bruise was just a rite of passage toward walking. Going for the BIG is all about your tenacity, your grit, your amazing ability that you are born with to get back up. From now on, every fall is just a fall. It's an opportunity to LEARN and get up faster, smarter, stronger, better than before.

Read our new mantra, just the first part. Falling down is allowed. That alone is probably a new outlook for most of us. I have seen bumper stickers that say, "Failing is not an option." News flash, people: failing is absolutely going to happen. We've been so hard on ourselves that when we fall down, we start beating ourselves up and continue to do so for extended periods of time. Feeling bad for feeling bad is insanity.

Look at the mantra: "Falling down is allowed; getting up is required." See, there's no time to beat yourself up. It's not part of the mantra. The mantra doesn't say, "Falling down is allowed. Stay down; feel bad, guilty, ashamed, and sorry for yourself. Then carry all that crap as you get back up." You didn't do that as a baby, so there's no reason to do that now. That's a bad habit you learned along the way to adulthood.

You learned that feeling bad, feeling guilty, feeling sorry for yourself was proof that you loved your goal, that missing your goal was important. That is not the truth. Feeling bad isn't a sign of how important your goal was. It shows an unhealthy relationship with falling down. We need to have a very mature, healthy relationship with falling down.

The next time you fall down, you need to be just like you were when you were a baby. You might cry a little bit because of the pain, but then you get right back up and you go again. From the time you were a toddler to now, you added to the mantra. The new mantra goes something like this: "When I fall or fail, I will beat myself up, mope around, and carry all this heavy negativity with me for the rest of my life." Wow, no wonder we think, "What's wrong with me?" This is really abusive to ourselves. You were born with "Falling down is allowed; getting up is required," and now you can get back to this truth and leave the lie behind.

After I got out of the Marine Corps, I went to college and played football. One of my coaches was a former marine, so we bonded over that. I had tons of respect for this guy. After a few games into the season, I felt I wasn't getting the playing time that I thought I deserved. I was working as hard as anyone else, and I brought the right combination of tenacity and violence to the linebacker position. One day after practice I pulled the coach aside to talk to him about the situation. I expected him to give me an explanation and encouragement and maybe console me a bit, but that's not what happened at all. I will never forget what he said to me. It is imprinted on my soul because it impacted me so much.

He said, and I quote, "The player in front of you is head and shoulders a better athlete than you."

Wow, talk about falling down; I was hit hard. It was like an eagle had swooped down and sunk its talons into my back. I was in the jaws of the bear, and I could not get loose.

It especially hurt coming from a man I respected so much. I went back to my truck after practice, and I just sat there in the driver's seat, crying. I had a tremendous passion for football, but if they didn't see my work, then I didn't know why I was continuing.

As I drove home that night, I asked myself, "What am I going to do about this? How am I going to get up from this huge hurt and failure?"

I was passionate about playing football, so I decided that I had invested too much to stop now. In my heart, I knew I could beat the guy. So I decided I would stay after practice and work even harder on my position. Anyone that came across me in practice was getting a beat down that they would not soon forget. I was known for hitting guys harder at practice than they would get hit in the game. I was on a mission.

The next week, my playing time didn't increase, nor the week after that. Then as the season progressed, I started picking up a few more minutes, game by game; and we were winning. We ended up being undefeated. We were up for the national championship. By the national championship game, I started over the player that I'd been told was "head and shoulders a better athlete" than I was.

\"Falling down is allowed; getting up is required." You can live by that; you can make that your mantra. Wake up every morning, stand up in a superhero position, and say, "Falling down is allowed; getting up is required." You will transform your life. Every fall you will embrace. Every fall you will know that that is part of the program, just like when you were a baby. Every time you see a baby learning to walk, it should reinforce what I'm telling you. It should reinforce the imprint on your DNA that "falling down is allowed; getting up is required." It's time to go for the BIG.

"Falling down is allowed; getting up is required."

https://www.themichaelbottsexperience.com/
http://l.ead.me/bavy8w

CHAPTER FIVE

There Is No Perfect

First, let's define *perfect*—it means having no mistakes or flaws. Perfection doesn't exist, yet we continue to struggle with the illusion of perfection.

Imagine the perfect love scene. There are two people with amazing skin. Their arms and legs are intertwined, and their beautiful lips are pressed up against each other. Their breathing is heavy and in sync. There's some music playing in the background as they giggle together. It's perfect, right? Now pan out and see the foot fungus, the cellulite, the smeared makeup, the armpit hair, the pimples, not to mention the smells. There is no perfect.

The entire world is made up of these so-called perfect scenes. After a lifetime of seeing them for hours at a time on every screen in our lives, we forget they are not real, and we start expecting our lives to be perfect in those ways as well—a perfect house, a perfect body, a perfect job, a perfect spouse, perfect children, a perfect business with perfect employees and perfect clients. I could go on and on. If we compare our reality to this illusion of perfect, we will always feel disappointed. It's a setup for frustration and disenchantment with going for the BIG and reaching our dreams and goals.

My amazing wife often says our wedding was perfect, and it was an absolutely fantastic wedding. My divorced parents came and got along. All the guests had a wonderful time. The music was a balanced mix of Hispanic and American music because my wife is from Ecuador. The food was terrific. It truly was a magical time for us, but it was not perfect.

Our photographer was below average. It rained all day. Several of the guests we were looking forward to seeing didn't come. The song played for the bridal entrance wasn't what we had chosen. It was the first wedding for the officiate, and he was so nervous that he was sweating more than I was!

Some of my family showed up late, and we had to delay the ceremony for them. It was anything but perfect, but because of what we chose to focus on, the good and the beautiful, it seemed perfect to us.

THE PERFECT TIME WILL NEVER COME

A 90-year-old grandmother was getting dressed for a night out with the family. Her grandson said, "Grandma, the kids and I want to know when you're going to wear that beautiful blue dress that we got you a few years back."

"Oh, I love that dress," the grandma said. "And I'm saving it for the perfect time. That dress is for a special occasion." A few months later, the 90-year-old grandma finally wore the dress, but it was at her own funeral.

There is no perfect. Now is the only perfect you get. Saving a dress for the perfect occasion, or waiting to start your business, or putting off the going to counseling with your spouse means you are wasting now and you will die of regret. You are too important! What you have to offer the world cannot wait. Go for the BIG now!!!

THE PARALYSIS OF PERFECTION

Some of us are waiting for the perfect moment, the perfect person, the perfect business, the economy to be perfect, etc. I'm not starting this business, because it's not the right time. We are waiting for the perfect time to get married or to have kids. People wait for the perfect time to start a business; we are waiting for the perfect time to quit our job. Just a little bit longer and it'll be the perfect time to go to college or to move to the new town.

First of all, whoever told you there was a perfect time? Nobody told you that. I am hard-pressed to find anyone that got married, started a business, went to college, had the kids, bought a house, or started a new adventure who said, "It was the perfect time, and that's why we went ahead and did it." There is no perfect.

If we judge our lives in comparison with everyone else's highlight film on social media, we will walk around feeling disappointed and sorry for ourselves because our life isn't perfect.

When my wife and I visit some of our friends, we see that their house is clean and organized and their kids are well behaved. It's perfect. Then she comes home and has a fit because our house is messy, our children fight, and the kitchen isn't clean. I try to remind her that those friends we visited knew we were coming and put a highlight show on for us just like we would do when people come to our house. If we go to their house on Tuesday at 2:00 p.m. unannounced, we will find that it is not so perfect. Judging ourselves based on other people's highlights only serves to kill our dreams.

The reason I can talk about this is because I'm an expert. I used to spend a lot of time comparing myself to the illusion of perfection, and it was destroying me.

There were times when I struggled to make payroll for my employees. I would beat myself into a depression because I thought I was such an irresponsible failure because I was struggling. Even though I always figured out a way to make payroll, my attitude toward the struggle was truly a tragedy for everybody. My wife, my kids, and my employees were all suffering from my breakdown of imperfection.

Finally, after a long stretch of depression and feeling sorry for myself, I learned from other business owners(show me your friends and ill show you your future) that struggling to make payroll isn't the end of the world and that I'm not a failure. I developed a mature relationship with failure.

Even colossal companies like Ford Motor Company and Microsoft at one point or another were challenged to make payroll, so I let it go. I let go of the illusion of perfection, and I fell in love with my imperfections.

WAITING FOR PERFECT IS EASY AND SAFE

Erin Baker owned Wholesome Baked Goods. Soon after she began making healthy breakfast cookies, she received a call from a woman asking for the nutritional information of the cookies.

It turns out the cookies were only two Weight Watchers points, and word quickly spread. In 1999 Erin's business went from two employees to 100 employees. Business was booming; everything was "perfect." Then Weight Watchers suddenly changed its point system, and in a period of eight months, the company lost 60 percent of its distribution. Now it was an "imperfect" situation.

Some people would see this as an opportunity to quit, because it wasn't perfect anymore because over half of her customers had left. However, Erin saw it as an opportunity to create new products. She moved her company away from the diet crowd when she realized they were a little fickle, and it's been successful ever since.

As long as we're waiting for perfect, we never have to take action. It's real easy to say, "As soon as the economy turns, I'm going to go for it. As soon as I have the perfect logo, I'm going to make those T-shirts. As soon as I lose this weight, I'm going to go sing at an open mic night."

It's a safe little cocoon where you never have to face failure. By trying to avoid failure, you have created a cocoon where you feel safe from rejection and risk. However, every day in that cocoon is another day lost. Every minute you procrastinate because it's not perfect is another day you are not giving the world all of you.

Not only is it safe and secure, that cocoon is complete selfishness. You've got your eye on three people when you stay in that perfection cocoon: me, myself, and I.

Whatever you're waiting for will not arrive in a perfect package delivered to your door. You must start now in spite of all the imperfections and the doubts and fear.

Let's look back at the love scene and at my wedding. Neither of those scenarios were perfect when we analyzed them, but at the moment when we focused on the lips pressed together and the intertwined arms and legs, it seemed perfect. When my parents got along and I was dancing with my brand new bride, it seemed perfect because the focus was on the beautiful. The focus was on the good, the kind, the sexy, and the generous aspects of the moment.

I know every moment can become perfect if we discipline ourselves to focus on the good and leave the rest out of focus.

This isn't ignoring the bad and the ugly. It's simply using our power of focus to zoom in on the good and the beautiful. Then when we go to solve the bad and the ugly, we have power and momentum to turn the bad and the ugly into seeds of good and beautiful. Ultimately, there is no perfect except to make now our perfect by zooming in on the good and taking an epic quantum leap of action. Now!

Social media has what I call the highlight effect; we see all the highlights of everybody's life and then compare our struggles and obstacles to their highlights. Then we feel discouraged and disappointed because our life sucks. WAKE UP!!! It's a highlight reel. Remember, there is no perfect, and when we scroll through these highlights, we are setting ourselves up for frustration, disappointment, anxiety, and depression. They're all highlights.

https://www.themichaelbottsexperience.com/
http://l.ead.me/bavy8w

CHAPTER SIX

Overcoming Negative Dialogue

When you are on an airplane, before you take off, the flight attendant gives a safety talk. In this talk, the flight attendant tells the passengers that if there's a change in cabin pressure, an oxygen mask will drop from the ceiling. They advise you to put your mask on first before you assist children or anyone else. What they don't tell you is that in seventy seconds you will pass out from lack of oxygen and then in about two minutes die and be of no help to anyone if you don't put your oxygen mask on first.

The cabin pressure of your life has changed, and this chapter is an oxygen mask. You need to put it on. Put it on first or you will be no help to anyone and you will die. Yes, die. The negative dialogue and anxiety that has you in a chokehold will cause death, death by regret—the regret of loss of love, regret of loss of opportunity, regret that you never found the courage to go for the BIG.

For a long time now, most every day I wake up with anxiety about the day, about my future, about my family. The negative dialogue goes a bit like this. Am I being a good enough husband? Am I being a good enough parent? It just keeps echoing in my soul. Am I being a good enough business owner? Am I being a good enough boss to my staff? Am I being a good-enough son to my parents? Am I being a good enough leader to the people that I lead? What if I fail today? What if I don't make enough money to pay my amazing staff? Am I serving God well enough? Am I living life to the fullest? It's pretty much a gauntlet of "am I enough?"

This litany of negativity is paralyzing, and it nearly destroyed everything I love and cherish. It is really a struggle to overcome it and break through to a place of confidence.

I have one mission. I am obsessed with helping you overcome the anxiety and negative dialogue in your life by giving you the tools and formulas I learned to break through with, so that you become a dominant presence on this planet.

We are not born with the anxiety and negative dialogue that bullies us into doubt and despair. As a newborn, we didn't worry. We didn't have anxiety; we didn't have negative dialogue. Somewhere from birth to now we have learned it, and we have allowed it to grow within our lives.

Anxiety is fear of not being enough now or in the future and regret for not having been enough in the past. As a child, most of us were told to be "good." But how would you measure good?

Is a C a good grade, or is a B a good grade? If I bring home a C, doesn't the conversation quickly turn to wondering how I can bring that grade up to a B? Then when I bring home a B, isn't the conversation still about how I could do better? So how do I know if I'm good?

If I walk straight home from school like my mom told me to, am I good? What if I take a different way home? If I still get home in the same amount of time but I took a different way home, does that mean I'm bad? If I don't eat all the food on my plate, am I bad? How do I know when I'm good at basketball? Is it when I make the shot? Is it when I can dribble? Is it when I can dunk? How do I know when I'm good?

48

You can see where this creates a state of uncertainty. A question starts echoing in our soul, a crippling, paralyzing query that lets the negative dialogue and the anxiety choke all the oxygen out of us and takes away our belief that we can go for the BIG.

Before we can get to the root, we need to clear away the dirt around the root that's covering it up. Here is some of the dirt that we've used to cover up this crippling question.

When things go wrong, we come up with some justifications as to why we can't go for the BIG. Here are two of the most common excuses:

- It's not fair.
- It's not my fault.

First of all, who told you it was fair? You're right! It's not fair, it never was fair, and it never will be fair. This "it's not fair" burden has been stopping you for too long. Right now you can let go of "it's not fair," and you can go for the BIG.

I know your burning desire to go for the BIG is too deep to let "it's not fair" stop you. From now on, "it's not fair" means it's not fair to the rest of the world, because you have an advantage. From now on, when you hear "it's not fair," I want you to spin it and say, "You're right. It's not fair. I AM ENOUGH. I am too awesome and too amazing, and I am going to dominate. I have an extreme advantage over the rest of the planet." That's what "it's not fair" means from now on.

Next is "it's not my fault." As long as "it's not my fault" is alive and well inside of you, you are powerless. You have given all of your power away. It's time you reclaim your life. "It's not my fault my business failed. It was the economy." Do all companies fail when the economy is bad? Did any other business like yours survive the bad economy? As long as you continue to blame the rest of the world for your current situation, you have given the rest of the world a free pass to play God in your life.

You are a slave to blame until you step up and take personal responsibility for your life as it is now. You will continue to be bullied by anxiety, doubt, failure, and negative self-dialogue as long as "it's not my fault" has a foothold in your life.

Michael, you are being unreasonable. What you are saying is unrealistic. Yes, it is. Your giving all your amazing power away just to dodge some personal responsibility is absolutely unreasonable. It's time you take your life back.

It's tough to take personal responsibility. The small you doesn't want to be responsible. The powerless you and the lazy you has an ego that needs to be coddled. As long as it's someone else's fault, we don't have to get up off our ass and go for the BIG. As long as it's someone else's fault, you have an easy way out. Embrace the truth of your brilliant power to take full responsibility.

Here's an example:but first let me say this: my grandmother, who I loved dearly, died of breast cancer. And one of my friends died from brain cancer at 39, leaving a 3-year-old son and a 5-year-old daughter, in 97 days after being diagnosed, so I know the devastation cancer leaves in its path. Don't miss the lesson here because of what cancer has taken from you!

My body is my temple, and when it's not working properly, it's my fault. If I'm overweight, it's on me. If my joints hurt, it's on me. If I get sick, it's on me. Okay, Michael, you've totally gone off the deep end. You are saying that if I get sick it's my fault. I need to take personal responsibility for that? Yep, because if I get cancer and it's not my fault, "Oh, I'm the victim of cancer, and I did everything all right, and it's not my fault." I have no power to influence the outcome. If I take personal responsibility, I smoked, I didn't use sunscreen, I ate fast food way too much, I didn't eat raw vegetables for a year, and I didn't exercise. Now that I've taken that responsibility, I might still die, but I know I have raised my chances of surviving because now I can do something about my circumstances. I can make drastic, ridiculous, unreasonable changes because the responsibility falls on the powerful limitless me.

You are too important, and your BIG is too important for you to be blaming others and not taking personal responsibility.

When you let go of "it's not fair" and turn your back on "it's not my fault," we can get to the root of the anxiety and the negative self-dialogue that's stopping you from your BIG.

Another damaging act is complaining. Complaining is like a riptide. Even Olympic swimmers can drown if they get caught in a riptide. It just keeps pulling you out into the ocean.

Complaining is a riptide pulling you out into the sea of anxiety and negative self-dialogue. Every time you complain, you give away your power and energy. You are building up the small you. Complaining builds momentum quickly like a forest fire and destroys everything in its path. Then, negativity fills your mind, and suddenly, you're on a roll of complaint and negative self-dialogue. Then, doubt, fear, and anxiety show up to feed on the complaints like a pride of lions on a zebra carcass. Complaining is a power move by anxiety and negative self-dialogue to keep them at the top of the food chain.

When has complaining ever helped you achieve a victory? Never. Nothing good comes out of complaining. It is a tough habit to break, but it will kill you, what you love and adore. Research has proven that complaining damages the part of the brain that solves problems. What causes anxiety? Not being able to solve problems. When you complain, you stall the brain's ability to solve problems. It takes discipline and focus to break this habit, but once you break it, going for the BIG will become clear and simple. In fact, your BIG will become small if you'll only stop complaining.

AM I ENOUGH?

At the root of all this anxiety and negative self-dialogue is the crippling question of "am I enough?" Am I enough to start my own business? Am I enough to be the parent my children merit? Am I enough to be the spouse my partner deserves? Am I enough to say something in this meeting? Am I enough to get the promotion? Am I enough to write the book and the movie? Am I enough to lose this weight and keep it off? Am I enough to get out of debt? Am I enough to get that customer? Am I enough to let my light shine?

Under all the complaining and "it's not my fault" or "it's not fair" is the painful, crippling question of "am I enough?" The scream of your soul questioning "am I enough?" is anchoring you to the bottomless sea of anxiety. Now it's time to remove "am I enough?" from your line of questioning.

For years now "am I enough?" has been your north star. This is the place from where you make most decisions. Now here I am reminding you that you are enough. "I AM ENOUGH" is the truth, but "am I enough?" has been bullying you most of your life. So I'm telling you that you are enough doesn't have much traction yet. Stay with me and be aware that "am I enough?" is under attack, and as you continue to take action with the success formula in this book, you are building "I AM ENOUGH."

"I AM ENOUGH" will get stronger with each action you take, setting you up to go for the big the way you were designed to.

GRATITUDE KILLS ANXIETY

Yesterday while I was in the shower, negative self-dialogue and anxiety started to try to take over, so I put gratitude into action. Right there in the shower I just started acknowledging everything I am grateful for. I said I am grateful for this clean water—it's very important to say it out loud. I am grateful for this tile floor I am standing on. I am grateful for this soap on my body. Immediately I was able to mute the negative self-dialogue and anxiety. With this simple but profound tool, I have been able to master anxiety as opposed to its mastering me.

THE FORMULA FOR WINNING OVER ANXIETY AND NEGATIVE SELF-DIALOGUE

Forgiveness is the first key to overcoming anxiety and negative self-dialogue. Typically, people think forgiveness is about the offender, but it's not; forgiving is all about the offended.

Let's say I steal a dollar from you and use it to buy a candy bar. You know I did it, but I will not admit it or apologize, so you become angry. I've already eaten the candy bar and forgotten about it, but you are still thinking about it. You think about it every time you see a candy bar. You think about it every time you see a dollar. You think about it every time you see me. How dare I walk around happy and worry free? How dare I even be in your presence? How dare I?

Do you see all the energy and power you give me by holding on to the offense? Forgiving is all about you. When you let go, you gain power.

A study was done where they measured the vertical jump of a person before and after leading them through an exercise on forgiveness. After completing the forgiveness exercise, the subject could jump higher. People become physically stronger from forgiving. Imagine the power you are going to reveal as you forgive. When I say you are powerful beyond measure, this is what I'm talking about.

FORGIVENESS IS A CHOICE

Most of us think that forgiveness means the offender gets a free pass, but that's not true. If I walk into a fenced yard and a dog bites me, I have a choice. Notice, forgiveness is a choice. I could sit outside of the fence, picking at my infected bite, and never let it heal. Or I can CHOOSE to get medical attention and stay away from that yard and that dog. Forgiveness doesn't mean you have to go back into the yard and get bit again. Forgiveness means you get help and move on with your life. Forgiveness is all about freeing yourself.

This is the time to be completely selfish and forgive every offense. Forgive the most terrible, horrific offenses committed against you, and forgive them for yourself. Take back the power and the energy you have been giving away.

Holding onto the offense is not evidence of how tragic the offense was. Forgiving the offense doesn't mean it wasn't horrific. The small, powerless "am I enough?" you wants to hold on to the offense as another reason why you can't go for the BIG. Holding on to the offense keeps the powerful you from coming out and changing the world.

Step one to muting the anxiety and negative self-dialogue is forgiveness. Please don't give up and decide that you can't complete step one or that you don't need to do that because perhaps you think what happened to you is completely unforgivable. You might be thinking, how can I forgive the person that raped me when I was 12 years old? Think about all the years from then to now and how not forgiving has held you back—not them, you!

I understand you might have survived some incredibly painful events. I know that it hurts, but trust me when I tell you that not forgiving has actually kept the wound from healing and prevented you from soaring into your BIG destiny. You have allowed the offense to anchor you in chains. You brought it from then to now, and it's cumbersome and burdensome. Now, at this moment, you have a choice: put it down, forgive, and soar.

Imagine how strong you will be now when you put it down. Don't imagine. Put it down and find out. See how effortless going for the BIG will become when you put it down.

HURTING PEOPLE, HURT PEOPLE

You need to know that "hurting people hurt people". If your parent neglected you as a child, just for a moment imagine them as a little child who was neglected. Imagine them sitting alone, wondering, Am I enough for love? Most likely if they knew better, they would have done better. Perhaps they never had any examples of how to be a parent or how to love; they simply didn't know how to cherish you. This exercise will help make quantum leaps in forgiveness and letting go. Again this is about you free, this is not about giving anyone a free pass.

THE THREE GATES

After we forgive, we then have to guard what I call the *ear gate*, the *eye gate*, and the *mouth gate*. I'm sure you're wondering what that means. A gate is an entrance and an exit. I call them the ear, eye, and mouth gates because you get to choose what you let in and what you let out.

One of the most secret, guarded places on the planet is called the seed vault. In it are 250 million crop seeds to help the human race rebuild in the event of a collapse.

You are the most precious and the most valuable thing on the planet, and access to you should be as secure, as secluded, as guarded as the seed vault.

However, we are so casual with our gates. We leave them open, allowing just about anything and anyone to have access. That lax behavior stops here. I want you to guard your gates. What you allow inside your gates has an impact on your anxiety and negative self-dialogue. If you allow gossip and negativity through your ear gate, that will allow anxiety and negative dialogue to grow. If you allow all the bad news of the world to come into your eye gate, you are feeding the anxiety and negative self-dialogue, making them stronger.

At this point you're probably annoyed because you're thinking that I want you to walk around without any news of what's happening in the world. Or you are worried that you will have to stop talking to your gossipy friends. My question for you is, How important is your BIG? How bad do you want to be free of the anxiety and the negative self-dialogue? How long will you settle for average when your BIG is at your fingertips? How important are the people you are supposed to inspire and reach and save? Is the news more important? Are your gossipy family and friends more important? I say NO! Guard your gates against negativity. Lock down your three gates like the seed vault.

Isn't it about time you got ridiculous? Isn't it about time you became unreasonable about your BIG? About your destiny? About your dream? Isn't it time for you to become obsessed and go for the BIG? You can be obsessed. You have permission to be ridiculously obsessed to go for the BIG. Your natural state from birth , your DNA is going for the BIG.

The Mouth Gate is the most powerful and amazing of the three gates. Right now, plug your ears with your fingers, and just say in a soft voice, "I AM ENOUGH." Do you hear that? That's called your inner ear. Every word you say goes in your inner ear. Then, your soul takes the message from your inner ear and starts to make it happen in your life. Just by speaking you have the ability to mute the negative self- dialogue and anxiety plaguing you. If you can grasp this truth, you can see that everything in your life is a result of what you've been speaking.

If you always say, "I gain weight just by looking at food," I bet you struggle with weight. If you say, "Money doesn't grow on trees. We always run out of money before we run out of month," then you inevitably struggle with finances. If you say, "I can never find any good employees," I bet you struggle with keeping staff. If you say, "The phone never rings around here," I bet you struggle in sales.

How about if we flip it? If you say, "My kids are so kind and generous," I bet you have people coming up to you to support that statement. If you say, "Business is great. I have a waiting list of clients beating down the door to do business with me," I bet that's what will happen. There's just no getting around this truth.

It's simple. Your words are incredibly powerful. When someone casually asks, How is business? I say my clients love me and bring me new clients. Your words are life or death!

"Only speak life into your life"

We have to guard what we say with the same seriousness that the seed vault is guarded with. That vault is guarded because the future of the world depends on having those seeds in the event of a catastrophe. Our words carry that same kind of life-or-death power. Once you realize that the universe and your soul are cocreators in making your desires into reality based on the commands you give them, then you will become excited about using your words to ensure only your most positive life manifests. Saying out loud "I AM ENOUGH" will create transformation.

Now that we know the truth of the power of our mouth, we are going to capitalize on that power.

THE POWER OF GRATITUDE

The third step toward muting anxiety and negative self-dialogue is gratitude. Being grateful has a profound impact on your body, mind, and soul. Studies have shown a 10 to 15 percent reduction in high blood pressure just from expressing gratitude out loud. That's as good as any medicine, with no adverse side effects.

Gratitude is a muscle that needs exercise just like any other muscle. It is a free super power that we neglect and keep buried under anxiety, worry, stress, and blaming others. We're going to change this forever.

Imagine you went to an appointment with the most respected doctor on the planet and she gave you a precious prescription that guaranteed you a healthy body and cured your fatal disease. Would you get that prescription and take it as prescribed? I would, and I'm sure you would too.

Now I'm going to give you a prescription, and if you become obsessed and faithful with taking the daily dose, I guarantee every single aspect of your life will transform—your body, your soul, your spirit, your relationships, your finances, your business. Here is your prescription: this is the tree of life!

Every waking hour say out loud with passion and energy two things you are grateful for followed by the statement "I AM ENOUGH."

Try this out loud right now: "I am grateful for my hands. I AM ENOUGH." After you say it, then take a deep breath and focus on how wonderful it is to have working hands. Then, do another one: "I am grateful for clean drinking water. I AM ENOUGH." You can be grateful for anything you want, and you can do as many as you like, but be sure to spend a few seconds every hour verbalizing your gratitude followed by "I AM ENOUGH." This only takes a few seconds.

Maybe you think that's ridiculous. You might be saying you can't do it every hour. You're at work. You have kids. You just don't have time. Really? You don't have half of 1 percent of an hour to spend making your dream come true? That is "am I enough?" making an argument to stay alive; no one is that busy. That voice telling you it's silly or you don't have time is really just "am I enough?" trying to keep you from your greatness. Do not let it win. You have to exercise your gratitude muscle by using it every waking hour. You have absolutely nothing to lose and everything to gain. Set the alarm on your phone right now, and start taking your gratitude prescription today.

BLESSINGS

The definition of a blessing is to revive a person with something good and desirable. The final step to muting the anxiety and negative self-dialogue is to bless two people every day.

One of the two people that you bless can be in your tribe, someone you see on a regular basis: your family, your friends, your co-workers, a check-out person at the store that recognizes you. The other person that you bless has to be outside of your tribe. They should be a random stranger with no way to return the favor.

Here's an example of what I mean about a blessing, based on what I normally do. I keep cold water with me as much as I can, and if I see a road worker or a postal worker or even my neighbors at my office, I offer them a cool water. When I see the janitors at the school where my kids go, I always stop and take time, and I say, "Thank you for these shiny floors. Thank you for the clean bathrooms." When you bless someone with words, you need to be very specific. If I just say, "Thanks for cleaning," it loses its power. But when I say, "Thanks for the shiny floors," I'm showing my gratitude. I'm blessing them because I'm very specific about their contribution. I look them in the eye, and I express my appreciation for their hard work.

When I'm in a restaurant and a uniformed officer or military person is behind me, I always pay for them. I love buying dinner for people anonymously. If I see a table of officers, I'm always hoping that I have the money to buy them dinner. Or sometimes at a toll, I'll pay for the driver behind me. I purchased a business from a man 20 years ago, and every month since, I've sent him a thank you either via text, email, or an actual card because that's how much I appreciate his helping me to start one of my businesses.

I send a lot of specific, personalized text messages to people in my life as I'm inspired to do so. Sometimes they're people I met years ago. I save them in my phone, and when I come across their number, I'll send a text and mention some detail about our meeting and how I appreciate them. Sometimes I ask how I could serve them. I often leave my wife a song on her voice mail. I send my grandmother flowers. I text my kids and tell them how proud I am. When I say I'm proud of them, I'm particular, not general. I say "I'm proud of how hard you work at your job. I'm proud of the grades you are bringing home." I don't just say, "I'm proud of you." That's too diluted and generic. I go out early on Wednesday mornings and give the guys that take my trash away each a $20 bill and express my gratitude for what they do. Imagine if they didn't take the trash away.

Now every day I want you to be in hot pursuit of two people to bless. Have fun with it and be creative. Maybe you can make it a game with some of your friends or family.

Of course, there will be days that you don't meet your goal. That's okay because remember that falling down is allowed, but getting up is required. Be obsessed with making your goal, and watch how your life will transform.

Regarding transformation, let me tell you what happened to Amanda. Her anxiety was so intense that she would often miss work because she was unable to get out of bed. Often she would need a ride home from work due to an anxiety attack.

When she asked for my help, she had been married to a firefighter for 15 years, and they had one son. From the outside, you would never guess that she was battling anxiety, negative self-dialogue, and panic attacks. She excels at every job she's ever had, and she's gorgeous. Her husband is handsome, kind, and achieving at his job. Her son is a valedictorian and a state basketball champion player. Her mom loves and adores her, and she's best friends with her sister.

Everything she touches prospers, yet anxiety, negative self-dialogue, and panic attacks were paralyzing her. She would miss her son's basketball games because of these panic attacks. She wouldn't be able to function as a mom or a wife. Sometimes her husband would have to take off work and help her get home because it was so bad that she couldn't drive her car.

This negative self-dialogue and anxiety had a choke hold on her for too long. The stress and the negative self-dialogue had stolen her joy and was damaging all of her relationships and putting her job in jeopardy. She asked me to help her, and I shared with her what I'm teaching you here. It's Important to note that she was ready for change and open to being coached.

As she went through this process, she began to see some incredible results. I remember her calling me in the middle of a panic attack. I asked her to start sharing a few things she was grateful for, and she was able to overcome the attack and stay at work the rest of day. That was a huge victory for her.

The anxiety and the negative self-dialogue weren't going away quietly. It was a bloody, physical, emotional fight. Amanda found the strength to win by being committed to taking her medicine every day—she performed her blessings, she acknowledged her gratitude, and she guarded her gates assiduously. If she called me and she hadn't taken her medicine, I would remind her that by giving the negativity space in between doses, she was allowing it time to recover and gather strength.

After a little while of coaching her, something happened that proved to me that Amanda and I were winning the war over her anxiety. Her husband told me that she was the happiest he had ever seen her in the 15 years they'd been married. Amanda began to experience the powerful truth of "I AM ENOUGH." That is what it's all about. You now have access to this healing prescription. Dedicate yourself to it and prepare for transformation.

I am writing this book to you so you can break out of the shackles of failure and defeat and sprint into your BIG with confidence and certainty!!!

"Am I enough?" will never entirely die. When it shows up, have it listen to your litany of gratitude and rounds of blessings, and watch it shrink into a weak shadow trying to avoid your light.

The reason this works is that your brain must listen to your audible voice. When "am I enough?" starts to bully you with negative self-dialogue and you speak out loud gratitude, the negative self-dialogue is instantly muted. Here's an example: Start counting in your head from one to 10, and then when you get to number five, I want you to start saying "I am grateful for . . ." Your mind stops counting and listens to what your voice is saying. The human brain is designed to stop what it's thinking and listen to what you are saying when you start to speak. You can't think one thing and say another at the same time.

When entertaining negative self-dialogue, you give it energy and power, and it will grow. But when you take charge and start saying what you're grateful for out loud, you instantly mute the negative self-dialogue. You cut it at its knees, and it loses its power.

YOU ARE ENOUGH

Right now, I want you to understand that you are enough as you are in this moment. You don't need to add or subtract a thing to be enough. You don't need to get another degree or take another class.

This is as real as it gets, people. We can mute the question of "am I enough?" We can take a scalpel and surgically cut anxiety and negative self-dialogue and panic attacks out of our lives if we take our medicine as prescribed. With this formula, you are about to embark on a life most people are afraid even to Imagine.

When you truly know that "I AM ENOUGH" as truth, your compulsions and addictions stop. They no longer have a place, because you are enough. When I know "I AM ENOUGH," I don't need to argue, because I don't even need to be right. When "I AM ENOUGH," how can fear entrap me? "I AM ENOUGH."

When "I AM ENOUGH," I can go for the BIG with confidence, conviction, and certainty. Failure has no power over me, because the concept of failure is all about missing something, and when I know "I AM ENOUGH," I know I am not missing anything. "I AM ENOUGH," so when failure shows up, "Okay, that's a failure. That doesn't mean I'm missing anything. That just means I missed that mark. I can learn and go again."

"I AM ENOUGH" is not jealous of someone else's success. You don't have to compare yourself, and you don't need to beat yourself up, because you know that you are enough. What would you say negative about yourself if you're living in a state of knowing "I AM ENOUGH"? You wouldn't say anything negative, because all negative self-talk originates from space of wondering "am I enough?"

"I AM ENOUGH" is confident in its limitless power to confront and overcome any obstacle. That's the kind of freedom you have in "I AM ENOUGH"!

I AM ENOUGH VERSUS AM I ENOUGH?

When you are presented with a challenge, notice the difference between what your voice of "I AM ENOUGH" versus "am I enough?" will say. It's going to be the exact opposite.

As you master muting the "am I enough?" voice and replace it with the confidence of "I AM ENOUGH," you will have to decide on going for a bigger BIG because the BIG you were thinking about previously will become as natural as breathing.

As you dive deeper into "I AM ENOUGH" and silence "am I enough?" "am I enough?" will do distracting things to stay alive and in charge. In "I AM ENOUGH," you are serving, solving and saving the world. "I AM ENOUGH" has a mission and a destiny and is in hot pursuit of it each day. "I AM ENOUGH" must create. "Am I enough?" has three people in mind and three people only: me, myself, and I.

Here is another resistance that often paralyzes us. In "am I enough?" you will not take action, because you need another degree, or the right shoes, or a certificate, or you can't, because "I don't have the experience." "Am I enough?" is always missing something, and that something is a hard stop to going for the BIG. So then "am I enough?" will spin this and say,

"Why are you reading that book? Why are you taking that class? Why are you getting that certification?" If you are "enough," why are you doing those things?

The answer is so beautiful and so brilliant. "I AM ENOUGH" is aware of space to grow and embraces that space without insecurity or vacillation. "I AM ENOUGH" takes action, takes risks, and attacks knowing there is always space and room to grow., the third step in the success formula is LEARN!

https://www.themichaelbottsexperience.com/
http://l.ead.me/bavy8w

CHAPTER SEVEN

Courage

Most of us consider courage as the absence of fear, but it's not.

Courage is action in the presence of fear.

Five men come upon a burning building. They hear a child crying inside, and one of them sprints into the building to save the child. All five men had fear. All five men had doubt and the desire for self-preservation. The one that sprinted in and took action in the presence of fear simply had courage and took action. Regardless of the type of battle someone is facing—physical, spiritual, financial, or relationship—the person with courage takes action regardless of how they feel. Taking action is what makes someone a hero.

Courage is not the absence of fear; courage is action in the presence of fear.

We can read about acts of courage or see them on the news almost every day, but rarely does anyone acknowledge the heroic nature of a single mom getting her kids to school and then herself to work on time. Rarely are couples lauded for the sacrifices they have to make to take in and take care of their elderly parents.

As I searched acts of courage, I didn't find many stories applauding the courage required for a business owner to start a company while putting four kids through college on their own or for the single father who takes care of his preschool daughters on his own. Rarely are these types of courage acknowledged.

When I looked up courage, I didn't find the story of an immigrant mother that left her 4-year-old baby girl and a 2-year-old baby boy to come to America and make a better life for them. Nobody toasts this woman, who's working three jobs day and night for years so that she can one day bring her children to their new home in America. I didn't find the story of a 17-year-old boy and his 15-year-old pregnant girlfriend that kept the baby in spite of the immense pressure to give it up. I didn't find the story of a young woman sneaking out with three kids in the night to escape her abusive husband. I didn't find the story of the 90-year-old man with the aching joints and arthritis that gets up every day and loves the ones around him. I didn't read about the entrepreneur that runs his business 12 hours then drives Uber for five hours, seven days a week to support his business.

You know why I didn't find these stories? It's because of the highlight effect. We see stories like those of Rosa Parks, Amelia Earhart, Helen Keller, and Nelson Mandela, and then we minimize our feats of courage. Then we go so far as to assume we are not courageous. This type of thinking leads back to the crippling question of "am I enough?"

You might think to yourself, "I didn't save the world today, so I'm average, just mediocre, and not enough." Meanwhile, you've been dominating fear, looking it in the eye and taking action anyway. Just getting out of bed and going to talk to a new client today is an act of courage. Facing rejection after rejection and keeping an attitude of gratitude is courage. When there is no money and you sell your van to keep your business alive this is courage.

You might not believe your courage is real, but let me ask you this, Why is it newsworthy when a woman locks her three kids in the car and lets the car roll into the lake and drowns them? It's not news when a parent gets up and loves the kids in spite of all the debt, the pressure of etrepreneurship and family drama. Why do we just let that go by as if it were nothing? This is displaying courage every day. The highlight effect has convinced us that the father who skips meals so he can buy soccer shoes for his child to play on the team is not displaying courage. Then we become convinced we have no courage and settle for average.

As long as we accept the lie "am I enough?" tells us, we will continue minimizing all our feats of courage. Then, if that weren't tragic enough, we go further and use the lie "I am not courageous" to settle for average in our lives. I mean, how could you go for the BIG if you don't have courage?

Or perhaps you don't believe that the examples I've given you display people with courage. Maybe you think all those people are just average. What if I told you there is no such thing as an average person? By deciding someone is just average, isn't that simply us judging?

Judging the choices of others means we are trying to protect our "am I enough?" voice of doubt. As long as "am I enough?" is dominating me, I am unable to recognize the courage of others. As long as I have the missing parts that "am I enough?" represents, I can never see the courage in others, because then I would have to see the courage in myself.

If I have courage, I must go for the BIG. It's safe to see the courage of the Wright Brothers in pursuit of motorized flight. That's a tremendous achievement. It's safe to see the courage of Helen Keller overcoming all her disabilities because I'm still safe and secure in my average cocoon. But if I recognize the courage of a couple taking in their mother while three kids are still in college, that type of courage is in my face. If I recognize the kind of hero that they are, then I have to be real and see that I have courage, and therefore I can and must go for my BIG.

For example, a man that just lost his wife and kids in a car accident might only be able to muster up the strength to sit by the side of his bed for a few minutes before lying back down. Then the next day perhaps he's able to get up out of bed and take a shower before returning to bed, because the emotional pain of the loss is just too great. Is sitting up on the side of the bed or taking a shower an act of courage? Without the backstory, it doesn't seem like it, but once we understand how much he loved and adored his family, then yes, it is an act of courage.

Once we pan out and see the whole story, we don't zoom in on what we think is average; we can see he's getting a little more courageous every day.

The only reason we would have any concerns about somebody else's courage or average is that we're trying to justify our own average.

Courage is just like any other muscle in your body. Start recognizing the feats of courage you are already doing on a daily basis. Then strengthen your courage muscle by using it, and spring into your BIG, knowing you are courageous.

DON'T APOLOGIZE FOR BEING A HERO

Most every day, I give some stranger a compliment on something I see in them. I see a man come out of the gym as I arrive, and I say, "Hey, great job getting to the gym today." After a recent high school football game, I shook hands with the policewoman patrolling the game and thanked her for making it safe for my family. There's a guy at church who puts the chairs away after the service, and I always try to see him and thank him for what he does.

Most of the time when I do this, the person I'm acknowledging minimizes their contribution. I get responses like "I'm just doing my job" or "It's no big deal. I'm just helping out." As long as "am I enough?" is lurking around, we can't be a hero.

This is just way too common. You are the most incredible, fantastic, beautiful, powerful, creative, toughest thing on the planet. Daily, you use your courage to face the world and life, and then you minimize the beauty of your effort. We have taken the concept of being humble, and we've twisted it into reducing all the awesomeness we achieve daily. Humility is lifting others, not lowering ourselves and diminishing our courage. All this comes from one crippling question, "am I enough?" If the statement were "I am not enough," we could challenge that. That's why "am I enough?" is so sneaky. "Am I enough?" is just subtle enough to create doubt, fear, worry, negative self-dialogue, anxiety, and panic. If it were, "I am not enough," we could fight against that, but since it's such a subtle question, it's almost like a ghost.

A hero has fear, but a hero can take action in the presence of fear. You are a hero and have been from the very beginning. You were born with courage, just like you were born with a bicep muscle. If you never use your bicep muscle, it will not develop. It will atrophy. Your courage muscle has atrophied. The good news is, courage degeneration is reversible. Just like your bicep will start to grow as you use your arm, the more you use your courage muscle, the stronger it will become. Your courage muscle has been neglected. Now that you're aware that you have a courage muscle, you can start to use it, and it will grow into this beautifully sculpted muscle that changes your brilliant ideas, your BIG, from a thought into an action and then a result that serves, solves and saves.

What is the thing you're afraid to do? What's been lurking in your heart and soul? You know what it is. I'll tell you what's happening. "Am I enough?" is screaming right now. "No, not that one. Pick something else. He'll never know if you choose something smaller." That's what "am I enough?" is screaming right now. Do you hear it?

However, this is the time to take action and exercise your courage. You have brought "I AM ENOUGH" out of hibernation. You have exhumed

"I AM ENOUGH" from the grave along with the clearness, focus, and tenacity that is your birthright.

Now put it to work. Put this book down, and courage up. Enroll in the class because you are enough. Make the call or send the email that you've been putting off. Do it this moment, for this moment. It's time to courage up and take massive action.

Sprint into the illusion of fear with your massive ax of courage. Swing your ax violently, cutting through fear and shredding "am I enough?" into a parade of confetti in celebration of a new, courageous you.

Right now, just say it out loud. Say, "I AM ENOUGH." As it travels through your inner ear, let it settle into your soul and become your truth. Then go for your BIG. The lack of courage to make a decision comes from fear of making a mistake. You were made to feel wrong or got the dissaproval look if you made a mistake or a bad decision.

The repetition of these disappointments created the fear of failure in making a decision. I'm here to tell you that you are awesome, right now, just as you are. Each time you courage up and make a decision, you're increasing the power of your courage. The only wrong decision is to not make a decision. When you don't decide, you open the door to "AM I ENOUGH".

Have you ever seen the money machine where a person stands in the glass closet and money is blowing around? They have 60 seconds to catch as much as they can. It's hilarious because most people end up with maybe one bill, but usually nothing, because they never decide which bill to catch. They try to catch them all and end up catching none. Making a decision is powerful.

I live near Washington, DC, and we have so many beautiful trees, which house thousands of squirrels. Often I come across dead squirrels in the middle of the road, and it reminds me that if we shy away from making a decision, then life will run us over.

Courage up and make a decision. Yes, you're going to make the wrong choice sometimes. However, it's better to be on either side of the road rather than dead in the middle after you've been run over by the tire of "am I enough"!

YOU CAN ALWAYS DO MORE THAN YOU THINK YOU CAN

I teach this statement in my talks. I teach it to my children. I try to live by it myself because I know that it is true.

My dad would always say when I was growing up, "The only limit you have are the ones you put on yourself." As I examine these two truths, the common factor is limiting beliefs. We need a to-do list, or a formula, to overcome these limiting beliefs. At this point we can all agree we have limiting beliefs, and those limiting beliefs have come from our history and our experiences. We've concluded, "I can't, because [insert limiting belief]."

Excuses are a result of the crippling question "am I enough?" driving us at high speed into the valley of average.

Here are some of the most common excuses:

- I can't because
- I'm too fat,
- I'm too young,
- I'm too old,
- I don't have the money,
- only men can do that,
- my family will reject me,
- I'm not good enough,

- I'm not smart enough,
- I don't have any time,
- I'm too short,
- my skin is the wrong color,
- I stutter,
- I have a learning disability,
- I have a physical disability,
- I don't have an education,
- I've tried everything and nothing works,
- I'll be rejected.

In the history of the world, has anyone who's short, disabled, broke, uneducated, etc. still reached the goal you're trying to achieve? When I ask you if someone has your excuse and achieves your BIG, that's in your face. Once you realize that someone else has achieved you're BIG while living with the excuse that you're letting stop you, then you realize that your reason is simply an excuse.

"Am I enough?" says "I've tried everything." Make a list of what you've tried. Be hard and true when you make this list, and you will realize you've tried about four to six things.

Thomas Edison had gone through 10,000 attempts before he succeeded with the light bulb, and we quit at four to six tries. When we say, "I've tried everything," our inner ear hears that. Then our soul and the universe go to work to make sure we can't achieve our BIG because we already tried everything.

With every excuse you say out loud, you give away your power. Remember, your words are life or death. Guard your mouth gate with high-level security.

Here is a great example. I was at the counter, paying for breakfast, and the server mentioned in the conversation she needed to lose a few pounds, because she just got back from vacation and she gained a few while she was away. I said, "Good job managing your health." She proceeded to say, "It's so hard to get back into my routine." She said, "I'm a runner, and I do yoga, and those are my things, but it's just so hard to get back into my routine."

I stopped her right there, and I said, "Try saying this. Say, 'It's easy for me to get back into my routine,'" and she did. She said it out loud. I said, "See, when you say out loud, 'It's hard to get into my routine,' you create a barrier, a canyon between you and your routine. When you say, 'It's hard for me to get back into my routine,' those words go in your inner ear, down in your soul, and now your soul is hard at work making it true . . . Your soul and the universe are going to create a canyon between you and your routine to prove you right. If you said, 'I love my routine. I'm excited to get back to it. It's so easy to get back to my routine after vacation because it's who I am,' your inner ear hears that, and your soul gets to work, making it happen." As we stood there, she said it a few more times. "It's easy for me to get into my routine." It was an aha moment for her. Your words are life or death.

RISK, FAIL, LEARN, REPEAT

Here is the formula I discovered after the desperate scream of my soul in that half bathroom.

Once this success formula was unveiled in my soul, I have used it to make quantum leaps into my BIG. Use it to expand your courage and transform "am I enough?" to "I AM ENOUGH." The ingredients are risk, fail, learn, and repeat.

First, let's look at RISK. The definition of risk is to expose oneself to a chance of injury or loss; to put oneself in danger, hazard, or to venture. With your new revelation that you are courageous, we can afford to take a risk. As you read the definition, notice the words expose oneself. What you've done before is you have covered up yourself with "It's not fair," "It's not my fault," "I'm too short," "I'm not smart enough," "I don't have the money." Those are all cover-ups to hide the powerful, courageous you. Now that you are free and liberated, the powerful you(I AM ENOUGH) can be exposed to welcome risk.

As the powerful you(I AM ENOUGH) rises out of the ocean of doubt, anxiety, and negative self-dialogue, you can embrace the uncertainty of loss, failure, or danger. When you know you are enough, what can you lose?

Remember, you can't lose what you don't have. When you take a risk, "am I enough?" will ask the question, "What If I lose that customer? If I call them and mess it up, I lose that customer." You don't have the customer; you can't lose what you don't have. Take the risk now. Failure is just an opportunity to get information. When you know you're enough, risk loses its venom.

"I AM ENOUGH" will take risks often in pursuit of the BIG. What is your risk today? I want you to sprint into risk with enthusiasm and excitement. Put this book down and take a risk right now. Make the call; send the email; quit the relationship; start the relationship; love with recklessness; go; move your body; eat the right thing; sign up for the class; book the trip. Remember, your courage needs a workout, so take a risk.

As your courage muscle grows, you will face higher levels of risk, and you're going to fail. In fact, if you think you're dominating risk, but you never face failure, you're fooling yourself and no one else. If failure isn't a huge part of your diet, you're not going for the BIG. If failure isn't an option, then it's not a risk. If I stand up, not much risk of failure. If I put 300 pounds on my shoulders and try and stand up, that's a risk because failure is a possibility.

Most of our lives we are taught that failure is bad, and therefore we resist it. I've seen bumper stickers and T-shirts that say, "Failure is not an option." That kind of thinking is fuel for "am I enough?" to use when failure shows up. Failure is a tyrant or a teacher. Failure will win every time we fight it. If we sit at the feet of failure and learn, then failure loses its sting. Failure becomes a teacher, and this is what became so clear in that tiny half bathroom when the water had been turned off. I stopped fighting and resisting, and I sat at the feet of each failure, hungry for the lesson.

Next, you have to learn; otherwise, you will become incredibly frustrated. When you learn from a failure, it loses its sting because it's just a learning experience.

What I've found is that if I write what I'm learning in the journal, I retain it better, and it gives me the power and courage to take a quantum leap into the next risk. Going back and studying your learning journal is the GPS to success.

The final piece of this courage formula is REPEAT. I coach a high school football team. When a player is practicing, I'm laser-focused on his technique and how he executes it. After the play, I sub him out, and I pull that player aside to talk to him. I talk him through what he did correctly and where he needs improvement. After our talk, all my players beg me to get back in to use their new knowledge. We need to be the same way.

As failure is teaching us, we should be so excited to sprint back into the game, going for the BIG. With our new knowledge, courage wants to go again instantly. "I AM ENOUGH," plus courage, always wants to repeat immediately.

Sprint towards the BIG with confidence in what you've just learned. You will find a way to breakthrough because you always risk, and when you fail, you always learn, and then you repeat.

I don't even need to put success in the formula because it is a natural result of the formula.

However, don't camp out at success. Don't set up a tent, build a cabin, dig a well, and sit around the campfire of success. Wherever you are right now, even if you're the most successful member in your whole family, you need to get back in the game; you need to risk, fail, learn, and repeat. Sometimes success is almost a detriment to going for the next level of BIG. Remember, success is a movement, not a stagnant location.

If you were raised in poverty, and now you live in a nice house, and you drive a nice car, you could get very comfortable there. You could become so comfortable that you ignore going to the next level of your BIG. You're not fully living if you're not going for the BIG. As soon as you can see that your goal is only one mountain top away, you need to start scanning the horizon for your next goal. I challenge you to continue to look into the horizon of the next big. The hunt is when you feel most alive!!!

I challenge you to take a risk today and every day. I challenge you to fail today. I challenge you to learn today, and I challenge you to repeat. The way you're going to do that is by being the hero, accepting that you're a hero, and exercising your courage muscle to

- risk,
- fail,
- learn,
- repeat.

https://www.themichaelbottsexperience.com/
http://l.ead.me/bavy8w

CHAPTER EIGHT

Your Pain Story

We've all heard someone say, "They said I couldn't do it. They said I was stupid. They all told me I was a failure and I would always be a failure." Who is this mysterious "they"? According to these quotes, there is an entire legion of people rooting against us, but perhaps the group of "they" isn't as populous as we first thought.

The definition of *they* is all people, many people, people in general. When we hear "they said I could never make it," we get this picture of a huge crowd or a mob yelling and screaming. If you're famous or running for office, this may be true. But for the rest of us, we probably don't have a "they" focused on our demise.

What happens is we have one or two people who say something to us that is not uplifting. Perhaps they've said it multiple times. Then the haunting question of "am I enough?" grabs hold of these negative words. Now here's where it gets interesting. We embrace this story, and it becomes a security blanket we use to stay average and never go for the BIG. I call it a pain story.

We take this pain story, and we frame it and hang it over the mantelpiece as a reminder of why we can't. Then every time we have a failure or we feel like quitting, we run back to our pain story and use that as the reason why we failed. The pain story is very comfortable. Or even worse we never even go for the BIG every time we get inspired and our passion for the BIG raises up we let "am i enough" hammer it out of us with the pain story

There are thousands of pain stories: My parents got a divorce. I've been called fat my entire life (your entire life?). I was beaten by my stepdad. I was raised in an orphanage, and no one wants me. My grandma has breast cancer; my mom had breast cancer, so I'm going to get breast cancer. Each of these and thousands I didn't put here keep us from going for the BIG.

You are not going to like what you're about to read. You need to proceed with caution. Be careful not to close up or close off. Transformation is about to happen, and the average you, the small you, the "am I enough?" you, is getting very uncomfortable.

Your pain story may come from a horrific experience that no human should have to go through. It might be monstrous and unimaginable.

I met this beautiful Asian woman who had been the victim of sex trafficking. She had been sold, bought, and raped from 8 years old until 22. At 22, she was rescued and went through therapy and treatment to try to cope with the tragedy of her childhood. I met her on her thirty-ninth birthday. We connected instantly, and she shared her dreams and goals. Weaved in her talk about her BIG was the tragic story of her childhood. My heart was full of compassion and love for her, and I admired her strength to have come so far. I also was clear that her pain story, of these truly horrific events that she had survived, was blocking her path to her BIG.

Even though I just met her, and it was her birthday, I felt in my heart that I needed to help her break free from her pain story. I asked her permission to tell her something from my heart. I proceeded to tell her that the only thing between her and her BIG was her pain story. She had told the pain story so many times; it had become a way out of going for the BIG. Whenever she was facing a challenge, she would sprint back to her pain story and give herself a free pass to quit or settle for average.

This is tough to hear. Are you using your pain story as a free pass to stay small and play it safe?

It took a moment for her to process for a reason that what I said was a lie. Then a lightness came over her, and she released this sigh of relief. For the first time, she had a way out of the maze of "am I enough?" She now had a map to her BIG. She just looked at me with tears in her eyes and said, "I never thought of it that way."

I told her that the horrific, inhumane experience did not make her special. What made her special was her survival. What made her special and unique was that she was here right now, breathing and alive. The courage to live another day as this was happening to her was courage few people possess. What she had survived could now be used to save others. The security blanket of her pain story could now be thrown off to reveal her in all the light of "I AM ENOUGH."

WHAT'S YOUR PAIN STORY?

Let's be clear, I know your experiences might be horrible and incredibly painful. Many people have had unspeakable acts committed against them. But the measure of how unspeakable your experience was isn't how long you are a victim of it or how long you continue to suffer afterward. If you recover the first day, or the hundredth day, or the thousandth day, that isn't a measure of how bad the experience was. It's simply a measure of your emotional relationship with pain and struggle.

You can take as long as you want to recover. You have permission to feel all the pain as long as you like. Remember, in "I AM ENOUGH," you have it; it does not have you! When you're ready, you can let it go. Now is always a good time. We are waiting for your brilliance. We need your light!

Your pain story is a crutch. "I AM ENOUGH" doesn't need a crutch. Your pain story has been a way to feel significant, to be special, to show your courage. I survived (fill in the blank), so I must be courageous. We don't have to go far to find someone with our same pain, or worse, that's living our dream. What we use as an excuse to stay in the muck of self-pity, someone else has used as fuel to rise and fill their life with joy, with peace, love, and prosperity, to serve others, solve for others, and save others.

I'm not saying that it didn't hurt or that it wasn't terrible or horrific. What I'm saying is that you forgot that you are powerful beyond measure. You forgot that you are limitless. You forgot that you are tenacious You can succeed because of and in spite of the pain.

Your pain story is not your final chapter. It's the introduction to an amazing success story that needs to be lived. You are stronger than your pain. Moving past your pain isn't superhuman. It's simply a decision.

The woman I mentioned before can courage up and save the lives of sexually abused children. She can be an advocate for them and change the entire face of that inhumanity. What about you? When you turn your back on your pain story, you will see the limitlessness in you. You will see and feel the "I AM ENOUGH" you were born with.

We thought courage was necessary only to overcome whatever tragedy we've survived. But actually, we need courage to embrace our awesomeness. Courage is for us to impact the world, for us to love our power. We have courage so we can shine our light so bright that the sun in jealous.

We might think the pain story is keeping you safe from failing, but it's not. Haven't you felt frustration, disappointment, and discouragement even while you embrace your pain story? Haven't you been hurt even with your pain story as the crutch for avoiding the BIG? There is no safe place. Your pain story is an illusion of a safety net. As you focus on your pain story and use it as the reason you do not go for your BIG, you will still plummet to the ground and be broken. There is no safety net!

Pain and struggle cannot be avoided. If you stay at the safety of your job and don't start your side hustle business, you can still get fired and be broke. If you stay in an unfulfilling partnership so that you're not alone in your business, you could still be left and end up alone. If you don't pay now with moving and eating some raw veggies, you will pay later in prescriptions and doctors' bills. If you don't go to open mic night because you might bomb, every time you see the ad for open mic night, the disappointment and frustration will be as real as if you did it and you actually did bomb.

Marianne Williamson says, "Our deepest fear is not that we are inadequate. Our deepest fear is that we are powerful beyond measure."

Our courage was put in us to face our light, not to just manage our darkness and our struggles.

We might ask ourselves, Who am I to be brilliant, gorgeous, talented, and fabulous? Actually, who are you not to be? Playing it small does not serve the world. There is nothing enlightened about shrinking so that other people won't feel insecure around you.

Sometimes we hide our light because we don't want to make someone else feel bad. As long we're living our pain story, everyone around us is comfortable. If we turned our back on our pain story and used our courage to climb as opposed to not falling, then we're going to start leaving people behind. Some people are going to choose not to be around us because we are climbing. It's not even a choice. Because they are stuck in not falling and you are climbing, they are just going to get left behind.

Mrs. Williamson also says, "We are all meant to shine as children do. We were born to make manifest the glory of God that is within us. It's not just in some of us. It's in everyone. As we let our light shine we unconsciously give other people permission to do the same."

To continue with the climbing analogy, let's say there's a group of people hanging in their courage harnesses from the side of "Mountain Go for the BIG," and their sole goal is to not fall. (They think their courage is to be used to not fall.) They focus their courage on their pain story, the past, when truly their courage is there for them to climb in the present into the future. Then if one person turns their back on their pain story and focuses their courage to the climb, some of the others might become inspired and realize they also can courage up and climb. Some people won't climb, because they will be convinced that you'll fall and it's better just to hang on.

"Am I enough?" distracts you into thinking your courage is to bear the past to survive your pain story.

As "I AM ENOUGH" is uncovered and "am I enough?" is muted, you realize your courage isn't to struggle to hang on the side of the mountain, but your courage is to propel you toward going for the BIG. Your courage has been facing the past, facing your pain story, distracted from climbing to higher heights. Wake up to this truth, and use all the courage in you to go for the BIG, to shine so very bright that the world takes notice.

Mrs. Williamson continues, "As we are liberated from our fear, our presence automatically liberates others." That is what we are here to do: liberate others, to serve others, to solve for others, and to save others.

BREAKING UP WITH THE PAIN STORY

Quitting the pain story is not easy. It may be the toughest thing a human can do.

Remember, if you don't turn your back on your pain story, you cannot save the ones you were meant to save. Use courage to do these daily, to be "I AM ENOUGH." Daily, forgive. Be selfish and forgive. Daily, guard your ear gate, your eye gate, and your mouth gate. Daily, say out loud two things you're grateful for, every hour. Daily, bless two people. Daily, take a risk. Make sure that risk has the possibility of failure, or it's not a risk, and then as you fail, embrace failure, sit at the feet of failure, and learn. Then repeat, faster, smarter, stronger, and better looking.

SHOW ME YOUR FRIENDS; I'LL SHOW YOU YOUR FUTURE

The final step of this transformation is to spend time only with people that lift you up and live the way you want to live. Who you are associating with matters. Returning to the climbing analogy, if you're hanging out with people who are comfortable just not falling, then that seems safe and acceptable. Once you start climbing and surrounding yourself with climbers, climbing will be your new normal.

Perhaps you can't get away from the people who are comfortable just hanging on. Maybe they live with you and you're taking care of them. Or perhaps you're married to them. If they're clinging to their pain story and they're connected to your pain story, you may not be able to help them climb. In fact, they may never climb.

My whole life I've been trying to bring people up the mountain that simply don't want to climb. Meanwhile, there's a whole world out there that does want to climb. If they don't choose to climb, there is nothing you can do. They're not the ones you're supposed to save. Someone else can inspire them; the best way to save them is just to courage up and start climbing yourself.

Right now, take a risk! Let's get you out of the "am I enough not falling?" cult and into the "I AM ENOUGH" climbing, risking, living tribe. Right now, take a risk. Your "I AM ENOUGH" inner voice is telling you the risk you need to take right now. Make the call, set up the appointment, enroll in the course, go for the run, and join the club. TAKE THE RISK!!!

You are going to run into all kinds of resistance and pushback from people in every aspect of your life. Everybody has been invested in your pain story, and now you are flipping the script, and it's going to create a whole lot of drama. Be ready for this resistance. Some will come along for the climb; others simply won't. Either way, you must keep climbing. We need you climbing, or we die. Our lives depend on you climbing, shining, and going for the BIG!

You have trained each and every person in your life on how to treat you. Now in the mindset of "I AM ENOUGH," you get to train them in a new way on how to treat the new you.

https://www.themichaelbottsexperience.com/
http://l.ead.me/bavy8w

CHAPTER NINE

The Currency of Success

I pride myself on being a free spirit, which is odd considering I've never drank alcohol or done drugs and I served in the United States Marine Corps. None of these things are in line with the stereotype of a free spirit, but I do love adventure and risk and being my own boss. I see myself like a wild horse, with no fences in sight. However, this perception of myself as a free spirit has been a detriment.

I notice that other people in circumstances similar to mine were racing toward their goals while I seemed to be stuck. I found this incredibly discouraging. These people weren't smarter than I was. They didn't work harder, yet how were they surpassing me? How were they eclipsing me in life?

Finally, I realized that my perception of myself as a free spirit and my attitude of self-discipline and being successful were contradictory to each other. No boundaries and no restrictions and having a to-do list to achieve my goal were in conflict. How could I be a free spirit and have discipline of a daily list of tasks to accomplish?

In my mind, a to-do list was a restraint, so subconsciously I resisted it. If I had a to-do list for a goal, the free spirit part of me would say, "Look how beautiful it is outside. Let's go play" or "You're smart. You can find a way to succeed without a daily list." I was in a civil war within myself, so I was unable to accomplish my goals. Then I would beat myself up and feel bad for not achieving them.

When I was in that tiny half bath with the stench of my life permeating my soul, this was at the core of it all. This civil war was killing me day by day. As in all civil wars, there were many casualties and collateral damage, including my goals, dreams, relationships, finances, health, and spirit; a peace treaty was in order.

The free spirit was creative and brilliant, while the self-disciplined marine was focused and determined. These two sides were locked in a constant battle. I transformed this internal battle by forgiving myself.

Forgiveness is such a powerful act. Decide right now to forgive yourself and free yourself. You need to love, embrace ,and accept all of your beautiful light. In "I AM ENOUGH," the world is really at your feet.

Instead of allowing my internal conflict to continue, I decided my self-disciplined side and my free-spirited side needed to find a way to work together. They needed a common foe that they could be allies against. I realized that common foe is the limiting question of "am I enough?"

The disciplined side believed that having a daily regimen and being focused was the only way to attack the day, while my free-spirited side believed boundaries create limits and mute creativity. The free-spirited side saw the daily to-do list as stifling and restraining. How could I harmonize these two opposing beliefs? How could I gain internal peace?

As I studied people who appeared to have mastered this dance between creativity and discipline, I had a major realization:
"The most disciplined is the most free."

Let this sink in a moment before you move on.
"The most disciplined is the most free."

Who is your hero? Who do you admire in any part of life? I admire a friend of mine named Michael Port. Michael has a beautiful life. Actually, I'd call it a dream life. He's in love with his wife. His business is thriving. He's a wonderful family man.

He has a wonderful home, a beautiful boat, and he's serving people with his life. He is also incredibly self-disciplined. His daily regimen is phenomenal, and it is within my reach. I don't see Michael's self-discipline as a superpower. I see it as absolutely attainable.

"The most disciplined is the most free."

A dear friend of mine recently passed away. His name was Jack Spencer. He was an amazing dad, a loving husband, and he had a thriving business. He paid cash for cars. He had paid cash for houses. His wife adored him. He had three sons who loved, respected, and looked up to him in every way. He had helped so many people achieve their goals. He was living my dream. He had the freedom to go and come as he pleased. He could afford first class, anywhere, at any time. He wasn't smarter than I am, and he didn't work harder than I do, but he was a master of self-discipline, and that self-discipline had created a freedom that few people enjoy.

"THE MOST DISCIPLINED IS THE MOST FREE."

As I matured in my relationship with failure, there was a residual effect. I also matured in my relationship with success. Most people see success as a destination; however, the truly successful have transcended this falsehood. The truly successful live with the understanding that success is not a destination, but rather, success is the pursuit of the dream.

You notice it's not getting the BIG, it's "go for the BIG" because the pursuit is the success.

Success is found in the pursuit of the BIG, not just arriving at the goal. Think about your last victory—wasn't the pursuit more satisfying than the arrival?

We all have a free spirit that thinks, "If I could live on a beach with no goals, I would be the happiest person." Many highly successful people have tried this, and they always end up back in the pursuit of a new goal. If they go to the beach and they just relax, all of a sudden they see an opportunity, and they turn it into a surfing tool or a bar that serves unique drinks. We are hardwired to create. We are created in the image of God. He is a creator. Therefore, logically, we are natural creators. Creating is in our DNA.

Success is not a destination. Some of us are suffering from the illusion that we are not successful because we haven't arrived. The highlight effect has tricked us into believing that success is a destination.

The screenplay writer thinks she's not successful, because a major studio hasn't picked up her script. The business owner thinks he isn't successful, because he still struggles to make payroll. The parent thinks she is unsuccessful, because her kid is a bit off course. The athlete thinks he isn't successful, because he isn't getting Division I offers. The college student thinks she isn't successful, because she is at a community college. The person trying to lose weight didn't lose three pounds this week, so they think they're not successful.

When I stopped hating, resenting, and running from failure and started embracing failure and learning from failure, then success wanted to be with me. Remember, failure and success are twins. When I started to ignore success and just dated failure, then success became obsessed with being with me.

This is another attempt at "am I enough?" trying to deceive you. Success is the pursuit of the BIG. If you're in the hunt, if every day you take a risk, then you are successful right now. Start seeing yourself as successful now.

REMAIN OPEN

There is more than one way to achieve your BIG. Sometimes we get so married to our idea, or our strategy of how to achieve our goal, when really what we need to do is open up. There is a way, but it may not be the way you had set in your mind. You need to open up to the universe and see other ways to grasp your BIG.

THE ELEMENTS OF SUCCESS

People often list hard work, discipline, sacrifice, focus, good friends, and accountability as ingredients in the recipe for success. However, here are some elements you might not have considered: giving, seeking, forgiveness, and embracing small beginnings and victories.

Giving

Giving is a principal part of the currency of success. Freely give money, love, respect, kindness, time, and anything else you have to offer.

How you spend your money and your time is a true reflection of who you are and what you value.

Seeking

Seeking is another part of the equation for creating the currency of success. You can ask for help, and in general, people want to help people. In fact, people need to help people.

Let's say you have to cross a minefield and you see another person who has made it across. You know that if you take one wrong step, your life will be over. Therefore, you should not hesitate to ask the person who has already succeeded in the endeavor you are about to attempt how they did it. Everyone who is excelling in their field has had someone who has helped them across the minefield of life. For example, Michael Jordan has natural talent and ability, but to truly exhibit his full potential, he has worked with and sought from some great coaches, mentors, and trainers. All the greats have overcome obstacles and achieved victory because they had a coach. They understand the value of asking for help and being open to receive coaching.

Embracing Small Beginnings & Victories

Another part of the currency of success is remembering to embrace small beginnings and small wins. As the highlight effect pressures us to achieve the astronomical, remember that everything that is amazing and beautiful started small. Look at you—you are the most amazing, phenomenal creation of all time, and you started as a sperm and an egg. Please love and acknowledge every small achievement with the appreciation that you are moving forward.

https://www.youtube.com/watch?v=yJzmPeKGlcY&t=39s

Often, if I ask someone to list their failures, they can quickly recite a laundry list of failures. "Am I enough?" has this list handy at all times to remind us of why we can't.

Yet when I ask them to list their achievements or what makes them extraordinary, they are often at a loss for what to say. It's important to recognize your victories, no matter how small you think they are, and learn to recognize them in others as well. In "I AM ENOUGH," we need to revisit our greatness, our list of the amazing, brilliant achievements in our history. This list is more evidence in the case of "I AM ENOUGH" versus "Am I Enough?"

Forgiveness

Forgiveness is another part of the currency of success. Remember, forgiveness is a selfish act to free you. The forgiveness factor frees you from the past and permits you to live in the now. Remember to also forgive yourself.

I coached a woman that had recently moved into a new home when her brother called asking to borrow some money. Immediately she felt guilty about having a new home while her brother, who had made some poor choices, needed help. Even though she did help her brother, that old question of "am I enough?" reared its head to make her feel bad about her prosperity.

After one of our sessions, my client was able to free herself from the feelings of guilt she was carrying around simply from having attained a goal that she had worked hard to manifest. It sounds ridiculous, but we all have done this.

Forgive yourself and let go of any regret or sadness you might be carrying. Release the could-have, would-have, should-have syndrome, because guess where all that lives—in the past, out of "am I enough?"

"Am I enough?" is not comfortable in the now. "Am I enough?" will pull you into the past with regrets and sadness, or it will push you into the future with fear and uncertainty. If you believe the lie "am I enough?" then you will be prevented from enjoying your new home, or new car, or new love, because how dare you have victory and joy in your life? "Am I enough?" says you don't deserve it or that it won't last. Forgiveness— true, reckless, unadulterated forgiveness—can only happen when you get the truth of "I AM ENOUGH." When it dawns on you that you are enough, there is no room for unforgiveness or resentment. "I AM ENOUGH" pushes these things out of your life.

Time

Another currency of success is time. Laser-focused time spent in the pursuit of your BIG is going to be tough. Everyone wants your time and attention. Also, when "am I enough?" is thriving, you will give your time away to please others. You give your time away to feel significant. However, once "I AM ENOUGH" gets momentum and traction, time focus becomes clear. Remember, the more disciplined you are, the more freedom you have. So as you bridle time and tame her, she will free you like no other currency.

Saying No

Another currency of success is simply saying no. No is a powerful currency of success. Imagine you are aware of the truth that "I AM ENOUGH" when someone asks you for some time that you have already put aside, dedicated to going for your BIG. You can simply say, "Thank you, but no" or just "No," and that's it. No explanation or excuses, just a simple no.

If you've been passing time out like free cookies and you start being firm with your time distribution, it's going to take a minute for all the people around you to adjust. I dare you to give it a try. You can still say no kindly, but lose the excuses and the justifications.

Now here's another spin on no. Remember the success formula, risk, fail, learn, and repeat? What if your goal every day were to get a no?

I had a client say that someday he was going to travel and teach dance and inspire people. His job was serving at a breakfast place, and the pressure of succeeding had paralyzed him and kept him from taking any action because he was so afraid of failure. I challenged him to take some action that day. Then I told him that what he needed to do was go out and get a no. The concept of getting a no freed him up from the fear of failure. He was not taking action, because he was afraid of the rejection. Once his only goal was to get a no, it freed him up to take action. It gave him the power to move and go for the BIG.

The truth is that if you didn't get a no today, then you didn't take a risk today. Get a no every day, and yes will chase you down. Imagine 365 noes. I'm not a fan of impossible, but being told no 365 times in a row is close to impossible. If every day you took a risk and got a no, I don't think, as long as you were learning, you could go 365 days and not have a yes/win at some point. I dare you to talk to a new person every day about your BIG. This works!

I had another client who grew her sales by more than 100 percent with the simple technique of trying to get a no three times a day.

Love

The number one currency of success is love. Love your journey, and love yourself. Love your BIG with so much passion and drive that you can only live in the pursuit of it. Fall in love with "I AM ENOUGH." Love the hustle. And finally, love the times when you fail. Failure is simply step two in the success formula.

THE STRUGGLE OF SELF VERSUS OTHERS IN THE CURRENCY OF SUCCESS

Sometimes I am so excited about the goal I have set my sights on that I try to bring everyone around me along on the journey of making it happen. However, sometimes these people have zero desire to go for this goal. Then "am I enough?" pops up, trying to convince me that if these people don't want to do it or don't think it's a good idea, then I must be wrong. After all, these are smart people I'm trying to enlist; they must know more than I do. This is just "am I enough?" trying to sabotage.

"Am I enough?" needs to bring everyone along, because if I'm not enough, then maybe someone else will be. This typically results in a short ride to depression, frustration, and quitting.

The people you were trying to get to come along are not bad people, but you have to understand that their opinion is not your truth. So let "I AM ENOUGH" be your guiding light. It's your goal you're going after. It's your journey, and it is unique to you. "Am I enough?" wants you spending all your time with these few that are never going to come along. It's a safe place. It's a small place. Let them go. Turn and face the rest of this big, beautiful world, serving, solving, and saving the ones only you can reach!!!

https://www.themichaelbottsexperience.com/
http://l.ead.me/bavy8w

CHAPTER TEN

Welcome to Your Beautiful Life

A REMINDER ABOUT FALLING DOWN

Remember, falling down is allowed, but getting up is required. You'll be fine. The secret is to rebound quickly. Don't waste time trying to break your fall or feeling bad that you fell in the first place. I challenge you to embrace falling down. Once you remind yourself that it's essentially your job to fall down and get back up so that you can serve, solve, and save others, then even the fall itself becomes part of your victory. Again, you have permission to fall; the important part is to bounce back quickly. This was a huge part of my demise. Every time I fell, I abused myself and felt bad for feeling bad. When I came out of the half bathroom and stopped fighting failure, I started learning from failure. Failure stopped bullying me and started teaching me. In "I AM ENOUGH," success was accessible. My BIG became clear and reachable in "I AM ENOUGH."

THE TO-DO LIST VERSUS THE DON'T LIST

I gave you a to-do list earlier in the book. Your tasks are to

1. risk, fail, learn, repeat;

2. forgive yourself and forgive others;

3. say out loud with energy and passion "I AM ENOUGH" with something you're grateful for every hour;

4. bless two people every day; and

5. get a "no" daily.

Perhaps you don't believe that you have time to accomplish this list every day. If that's what you're thinking, then "am I enough?" is still in charge of you.

Ultimately, if you truly want to manifest your BIG desire, you'll be excited to experiment with this to-do list and even go for extra credit!

You deserve to win, so just know that you can expand your capacity to fit these exercises into your life, and be excited to see the results. Otherwise, you are still living under the delusion that your breakthrough isn't worth the effort. Trust your desire, and know that you are enough to accomplish it.

The mindset of "I AM ENOUGH" will naturally take a risk every day. An "I AM ENOUGH" mentality will embrace any potential failure resulting from a risk you took in pursuit of your BIG. If you're secure in the knowledge of "I AM ENOUGH," you can embrace the repetition of learning and forgiveness. When you live in the world with the confidence of "I AM ENOUGH," you are truly grateful, and you want to share that feeling through blessing others. Your life becomes a beautiful symphony that you are conducting. In "I AM ENOUGH," time is in you. You make time just like you make money. "I AM ENOUGH" creates. You see the world around you, and you are aware of opportunities to bless. "I AM ENOUGH" can accomplish more in 90 minutes than "am I enough?" can in eight hours. "I AM ENOUGH" is laser focused, cutting through doubt, fear, anxiety, and limiting beliefs.

TO-DO AND TO-DON'T

Here is a continuation of steps to take toward achieving your BIG, along with some pitfalls to avoid.

- Remember to guard your gates: eyes, ears, and mouth. Only allow positive and inspirational information into your gates, and guard against negativity entering your brain.
- Only associate with people that are also on a mission to achieve their BIG. Do not spend time with people who are stuck in a cocoon of average.

CHASING NO

In one of my talks, I taught the concept of going out to get a no every day. The very first day my client tried it, she called to report that she had received five yeses! The day after our session, she approached five different people that she knew peripherally and offered to give them an estimate. Because she was living in the momentum of "I AM ENOUGH" and was convinced that she could handle receiving a no, she was able to attract five yeses. Before, when she was still questioning whether she was enough, she felt too vulnerable to risk receiving a no because that would validate every doubt she had about herself or her career. Meanwhile, she had been working hard within the same field for 13 years, and every day she tried to get a yes. But it wasn't until she applied the steps I've shared with you that she was able to pull in five yeses in one day. That is the power of going for a no.

IDENTIFYING YOUR BIG

I was sitting at a restaurant by myself, and next to me was a woman named Allison. I had never met Allison, but we struck up a conversation that went something like this:

Me: What do you do for money?

Allison: [Laughing] I never been asked quite like that. I work at a dental office Monday, Wednesday, and Friday to pay the bills.

Me: What's your passion?

Allison: I don't know . . .

Me: Of course you do.

Allison: People have said that to me before, but I do not know.

Me: Allison, what's really going on is your passion is so scary you don't want to say it out loud. You know what it is, but saying it out loud is just too scary.

She sat on the edge of her seat and leaned into my words. Then with a trembling voice, she said,

"I want to be a novelist."

Her body language was scared and relieved at the same time.

Me: Have you started writing yet?

Allison: Oh yes. I write on Tuesday and Thursdays.

Me: I am confused. It sounds like you are already a novelist.

Allison: Well, I want to get paid for my writing.

Me: So your passion you didn't know a minute ago is to get paid for your novel?

Allison: Yes.

Me: What's your novel about?

Allison: My story is about Zombies. And with the popularity of *The Walking Dead*, my story would not be a success.

Me: How many hamburger joints do you think there are within a mile of us right now?

Allison tilted her head like a cow looking at a new gate.

Allison: I don't know, maybe 20.

Me: Yes, there are about 20 hamburger joints within a mile of us because everybody likes hamburgers, but they all like them a little different, just like zombie lovers will want a different flavor of zombie than just *The Walking Dead.*

Allison got very excited with a newfound passion and fire for her BIG goal. Immediately she lit up about the possibility of being a paid novelist.

In your heart, you know what your passion is, your BIG. Now it's up to you to courage up, cut through fear, and state out loud with confidence, conviction, and certainty.

If you were guaranteed success, what would you do? What would be your BIG? If there were no limitations of any kind—not your age, weight, sex, race, income, past, or level of education—what would be your goal? The answer to that question is your BIG. That's what you can manifest with the success formula—risk, fail, learn, repeat.

You are a miracle. You showed up in the exact perfect time, in this spectacular human form, to impact the world in a way that only you can. There has never been a you in the history of time; there will never be a you in the future of time. You are so unique, you are so special, and only you can do what you can do for the world right now. If you don't do it, people are going to die.

I have a client who's an organizer, but she's still living under the weight of "am I enough?" Finally, I had to give her an example to wake her up to the power of the service she provides and her ability to impact the world.

I gave her a scenario where a client is overwhelmed by the disorganization in her house, and it kept her from being fully present with her kids. Perhaps her distraction by trying to manage her out-of-control home and life could contribute to missing signals from one of her kids that they were struggling. What if that kid took his or her own life?

Now what if that mom had become her client and was able to keep her life in order? Perhaps just that adjustment would result in keeping that kid alive.

Once you truly understand that your life, and the life of an untold number of others, depends on your achieving your goal, then you don't have time to care what others think. You cannot spend any energy worrying about failing. If you stop to complain or blame, others will die.

When you are drowning for your BIG, your focus becomes life or death in intensity. When you're swimming toward the surface, you are on one mission, and no one and nothing will stop you. You know you can and must make it to the surface, but you have to summon all of your strength in order to make it. You are under the water, and your lungs are screaming for air, your arms and legs are exhausted, but somehow you fight on because the only other option is death.

When you're drowning for your BIG, finishing is easy. Bursting through the surface and taking that breath of life will happen. I guarantee it. But you must have a burning desire. It has to be everything to you.

I'm telling you, you are enough as you are this moment to go for your BIG. You do not need another class, you do not need to read another book,(except this book you need to read this book) and you do not need to get the right shoes before you start running or the right dress before you return to dating. You do not have be certified in something else to go for your BIG right now. Start as you are now!

It is fine if you do get the shoes, or take the course, or lose the weight, but start right now, going for your BIG. You are enough to go for your dream. You can add or subtract those things as they come, but do not let anything delay or paralyze you from taking action toward your goal now.

If you think you need something that's outside of yourself, then that means "am I enough?" is alive and well in your life. You must go now because the people that you have to save need you now. They can't wait for you to get another certification or lose 30 pounds. The people that are in the dark, about to go blind, can't wait another day for you to shine your unique light on them. You have to shine your light right now.

Going for the BIG is a struggle. We all need the struggle to break out of the cocoon of average. You are a butterfly, and your wings will not develop if someone cuts you out of the cocoon from the outside. You must fight your way out to develop your wings. Now that you know the benefit of the struggle, you can embrace it. Use your struggle to assure people that they, too, can overcome their struggle. Then, as the beautiful butterfly you are, you can pollinate the world with your bright light and save the ones only you can save.

As I mentioned before, each of us are creators. We are created by God in his image. He is a creator. Therefore, logically, we are creators. You are going to create something out of nothing. You do not have a choice. But what you create is a choice. When you're living in "am I enough?" you create drama, strife, and stress for others and yourself.

My wife had taken my name off the Costco card membership, and I needed to get some old 35 mm film developed, and she was busy. I started to create something out of nothing and started rehearsing what I was going to say and got all stirred up and angry. "How dare she take me off the membership?" I was letting "am I enough?" take over and create drama. I snuck into Costco, still fired up at my wife—this was all her fault (note that the blame game was being played). Then I find out that Costco doesn't even process 35 mm film anymore!

Another time I missed a call from an old colleague, and I thought, Why he is calling me? I had a project that was slightly related to something he and I had worked on in the past. My first thought was, Is he calling me to fight over this dead project that I revived? I went into all this drama about it and how I was going to handle it. "Am I enough?" was sabotaging my good vibe about the project. I was actually scared to call him back because of all the scenarios I played in my head. I came out of that after 20 minutes and just called him. It turned out it was nothing but a friendly reach out. We are all guilty of this at some point. It's creating something out of nothing.

I have wanted to write this book for a very long time, and my soul was screaming for me to take action. But I was allowing "am I enough?" to lead me down the path of non-action for fear of failure. "I AM ENOUGH" got traction and became strong and powerful because I took my medicine daily. You are reading something that was created out of nothing. Every entrepreneur has used the power to create something out of nothing, to create good in the world.

This is your wake-up call: No more average. No more settling.

Be you; you are a gift to the planet.
Be you, and inspire the world.
Be you, and save the world.
Be the you that lives in "I AM ENOUGH."
Be the you that lives in going for the BIG.
Be you, and sprint into risk, fail, learn, and repeat.

I believe in you. Reach out to me. I want to get to know you and see your BIG change the world. TheMichaelBottsExperience.com

©MichaelBottsLLC

https://www.themichaelbottsexperience.com/
http://l.ead.me/bavy8w

Made in the USA
Middletown, DE
18 January 2019